REMINISCE
GRIMSBY TOWN FC
1879-1912

by Bob Lincoln

extracted from

Reminiscences of Sport in Grimsby

(Published 1912)

British Library Cataloguing in Publication Data
A catalogue record for this book is available from the British Library

ISBN: 978-1-86223-082-8

Copyright © 2003, SOCCER BOOKS LIMITED (01472 696226)
72 St. Peter's Avenue, Cleethorpes, N.E. Lincolnshire, DN35 8HU, England
Web site www.soccer-books.co.uk
e-mail info@soccer-books.co.uk

This third impression published in 2017.

Printed in the UK by 4edge Ltd.

INTRODUCTION

Extracted from his book 'Reminiscences of Sport in Grimsby' which was published shortly before his death, this is Bob Lincoln's personal account of life in football with his beloved Grimsby Town. A leading figure at the time of the club's formation in 1878, he served the club first as a player then as a benefactor, director and finally, through this text, as an historian.

However, this is more than just the story of Grimsby Town football club in the early years – it's amusing, irreverent, informative and simply a cracking good read which could be about almost any small town Football League club around the turn of the century. Even now, amazingly, many of Bob's observations about the world of football are so relevant that they could have been written yesterday!

When Bob's book was first published in 1912, it was commonplace for advertisements for local businesses to be interspersed throughout the text. We have included a selection of these fascinating advertisements in this book for a number of businesses, some of which still trade today!

Photo by]   [Sherlock, Grimsby

Faithfully yours
Bob Lincoln

THE AUTHOR TO THE READER.

IT is somewhat a novelty to be a walking encyclopaedia, yet without boasting particularly I can conscientiously say that for a number of years, quite a decade, it has invariably been the rule if any knotty question or argument arose *re* the date or result of any particular match, either cricket or football, or anything pertaining to manly sports, Bob Lincoln was appealed to, and it is no exaggeration to state my decision has decided hundreds of bets. Speaking of this to my friend Mr. J. M. Tierney, of Green Lamp fame, he said, "Why on earth don't you write your Reminiscences of Sport in Grimsby." Hence to a great extent the appearance of this effusion, which I am inflicting upon you. Whether it is quite up to the mark from a journalistic point of view is quite immaterial to yours truly, but you can take it from me that I have endeavoured to the best of my ability to give a true history of my reminiscences in the sporting world during the period of approximately half a century. With not a few, possibly some of the yarns may appear a bit tall, but I can assure the reader everything is chronicled as it transpired, and I would appeal to those who care to wade through these pages not to be too harsh in their criticisms, and above all to remember it is the puerile effort of a novice. In the numerous references to players and officials possibly a stray note may have caused offence, but if so, I can assure them it has been the furthest from my thoughts. Indeed, if there is one thing in particular I have endeavoured to avoid it is to write anything of an offensive description. Perhaps it may be just as well to mention that I may be accused of what is commonly known as blowing the horn on my own behalf. If I have occasionally it is a common fault. In fact in these days of keen competition it would indeed be a novelty to find any individual do it on your behalf, therefore possibly it is a fault in the right direction. In compiling this brief resumé of sport, I can truly say it has been a labour of love. Reminiscences crowded on me so speedily that the bulk of it was done well within the month, principally from memory. Don't imagine, however, for a moment, that I have not cocked my neb over files of newspapers for statistics and other matter. This would clearly be an erroneous idea. Indeed, I was reminded more than once of the Jester in Sullivan's "Yeoman of the Guard," when he does the impromptu dance, book in hand. Before concluding, may I thank all those kind friends (particularly G. Skelton, Esq.), and they have been very numerous, who have so generously assisted me in my efforts. Throughout I have been received with the greatest courtesy by the various secretaries and officials of the clubs, and it has indeed been a pleasure to me to note the alacrity with which many of the members have faced the camera, and thus enabled me to have thoroughly representative groups in the book. In conclusion, however agreeable the compiling of it may have been, I should imagine the majority of the readers will not be surprised to hear that it was with a sigh of relief I affixed the simple word

FINIS.

FOOTBALL

FROM 1879 TO 1912.

Clearly the most popular pastime of the day. Well do I remember away back in the early seventies when a few of the old hands (the bulk of whom are still in the land of the living as a casual glance at the old brigade group will prove), endeavoured to bring it to the front. How we were laughed at, but yet those who jeered at our efforts, within say a couple of years, were present round the ropes frantic in their enthusiasm, in fact there was a genuine ring about it quite different to that of the present day. Only those who have been in the know throughout the rise of the game can realise the gigantic strides made in the pastime. The reasons are obvious. Firstly, that grand achievement of the British workman, namely, the half-day holiday on the Saturday, is undoubtedly the keystone. Secondly, the period of play is brief. You are certain of a game bar anything short of earthquakes, likewise a definite result, an item of immense importance. Possibly to the late Mr. McGregor, the canny Scot, who initiated the League system, the credit is due for its present prosperity, but others have played a great part in that all necessary portion of the programme, keeping the various clubs under control, namely, Lord Kinnaird, Major Marindin, W. E. and C. Clegg (Sheffield), and other gentlemen I could mention against whom ne'er a breath of suspicion has been made. In the near future the various directors have a difficult problem to solve. To the average spectator everything looks bright to a degree, for have we not everything quite up-to-date. At the commencement of the season, look at the team, smart in their new colours, stands freshly painted, in fact to sum it up briefly an air of prosperity is apparently to the front to the casual spectator, but to those not in the know I would point out that invariably there is a gaunt spectre knocking about, which only those who have been through the mill can realise. Look at the average Director's face, clearly it is a study, and not without reason. During the close season he has been responsible for a large sum of money, the return of which can only be assured by the good form of the team. Will they crack up on their initial effort, or will the form shown realise their expectations. Truly this is a knotty problem, and you can take it from me that the director of any first-class club instead of being consigned, well not to Cleethorpes, is deserving of the gratitude of all the spectators, for his efforts to provide them sport of an attractive character, and likewise the pecuniary risk he runs in being the proprietor of the bird whose struggles to exist I have endeavoured to pourtray in the following record of Grimsby Town. And now what about the players? Who is invariably with the average spectator, either a god or otherwise. Without speaking disrespectfully of those in the early days, clearly there is a better tone in the class, in a great measure attributable to the fact that it has become recognised as a profession, and persons having already a social position in the world, such for instance as the scholastic profession, have not hesitated to abandon this for the precarious one of the footballer.

Naturally this, amongst other causes, has been the means of raising the wage list to the extreme limit, in fact in the immediate future something drastic will have to be done or the bulk of the clubs will have to write Ichabod over their portals. Never a pessimist, yet I would point out that the clubs actually solvent can be counted without troubling double figures, and the bulk of these simply because those at the helm have the sense to buy their own freehold. It is satisfactory to note this is recognised by the Football Players' Union, and therefore there is every prospect of some plan being formulated, which will enable the bulk of the clubs to weather the storm, and thus be enabled to satisfy their patrons without the Directors being responsible for the heavy liabilities they are liable for at the present day. I cannot conclude this opening epistle on the Winter pastime without referring to that class of spectator, alas so prevalent on every ground of note, who are in their element when possibly the team, through no fault of their own, are having that run of bad luck experienced by every club. How easy it is to throw the arrow of suspicion. The favourite expression being possibly that somewhat common, yet expressive word, "booze." What utter rot; I don't say a player may not lift his elbow occasionally, they are but mortal, but you can bet your bottom dollar that he is very soon a marked man in the football world. Yes, the rules are too drastic to allow this to exist, and briefly speaking, at the present day, considering the temptations he has, the average professional will compare favourably with any other individual whether on the playing field or not.

Left to Right—W. T. Lauwin, R. C. Hall, Bob Lincoln, G. Atkinson, H. Evans, W. Ashling, A. H. Read.

S. Noble, J. Warner, T. Atkinson, H. Monument, J. Fanthorpe.

GRIMSBY PELHAM F.C., 1878.

9

HOUSEHOLD COAL

STEAM AND NUT COAL

SUPPLIED FROM THE FOLLOWING RAILWAY DEPOTS :—

Cressey Street, W. Shaw, Foreman.

Humber Street, H. Plumtree, Foreman.

Railway Street, G. Clayton, Foreman.

Cleethorpes Station, J. Humberstone, ,,

ED. BANNISTER & CO., LTD.,

FITTERS TO THE ADMIRALTY.

ROYAL DOCK CHAMBERS.

TELEPHONE No. 10.

Who said Coke Ovens? Possibly to the rising generation in the Fisheries the position of this salubrious locality is a myth, and yet in close proximity to them in the early sixties both cricket and a primitive kind of football was the order of the day. They were situated near the Dock Station, and it was on the pastures the other side of Railway Street, where athletes indulged in the various pastimes.

With the majority of the followers of the game the idea is prevalent that Grimsby was about the first town in the county to adopt football, but this is quite an erroneous idea. As a matter of fact it was practically the last, and long ere it became prominent in the Fisheries strong clubs had been formed in Spilsby, Lincoln, Grantham, Brigg and even Louth. True, I myself and any amount of others I could mention played the game in the streets, with the goals in embryo, slightly more apart than the orthodox distance, as, for instance, one used to be in Pasture Street, where Hewitt's Offices are, and the other against King Street, Cleethorpe Road. Yes, we youngsters had a rollicking time in the old days. We practically took possession of the streets. There were only about haf-a-dozen policemen with Ikey Hansen (who fiddled the ham) as chief, and they were never in a particular hurry. What do you think?

Speaking from memory I don't think that any club of note to play a series of matches was formed before 1879. To this day it is a difficult problem to decide which really was the first club, the Pelham, White Star, or the Wanderers. Each has its partizans, but personally I am of opinion that the Pelham should have had the credit. The latter club had its ground just beyond Phelps Street, New Cleethorpes, the White Star the adjoining field, although they originally played on the sands, whilst the Wanderers disported themselves on a piece of pasture land in the Marsh, near where the Grimsby and District Hospital stands.

Of course I am open to correction, and at this period when I am about commencing to inflict my crude remarks on the game upon my readers who may care to read them, I should like it to be known that it is not my intention to introduce anything of a personal character. I shall endeavour to make a fair comment on the ability of the various clubs and players, and the officials connected in the working of the clubs will not be named in full, but will have to be content with hieroglyphics.

Left to Right—A. H. Read, R. C. Hall, Bob Lincoln, F. Marshall, J. Warner, A. Ousey, W. T. Lammin.

S. Noble, H. Monument, J. France, T. Atkinson, F. Lowe.

FIRST TOWN FOOTBALL TEAM, 1879.

The match I referred to up aloft was the Pelham versus Louth, played upon the Town ground, on the 1st of November, 1879, which resulted in a drawn game, the score being one goal each. Evidently it was exciting enough as the visitors equalised in the last minute. The following were specially mentioned as playing well :— Grant, Unett, Horn (the present master at Welholme Road School), and Barker (Clerk of the Peace). Of course other matches were played by the Pelham. I myself played in them, but it was not until the following year when, in my opinion, other clubs were played by either the Wanderers or the White Star. They met twice, the White Star winning the first match by three goals to one, and the Wanderers the second by three goals to two.

In the meantime the Pelham had been merged into the Town Club and amongst the matches played was one with Louth, which one player in particular had reason to remember, viz., Tom Atkinson, who had the misfortune to have his collar bone broken — about the first accident I can remember in the football field.

With not a few the idea is prevalent that the playing of three half-backs is comparatively of recent date, but for their information I can tell them that both the above clubs occasionally played them, and this upwards of thirty years ago.

For the season 1881-2 Grimsby Town arranged quite an ambitious programme, running two teams, the second being known as the Wanderers. The first had fixtures with Hull Town, Louth Town, Brigg Town, Barton, Spilsby, and Basford Rovers, whilst the Wanderers met Hull Dairycoates and M. S. and L. (Ironsides), etc. It may surprise not a few to find Hull Town amongst the fixtures, but just then they had a powerful team, consisting principally of Hull Town cricketers, a far stronger team by-the-bye than the one that played the Grimsby Rovers last Summer.

I well remember the first time I played against them, the ground was situated on the Boulevard, between Hessle and Anlaby Road. It had several peculiarities in it. One I have never seen on any other ground, inasmuch as on the playing portion there was quite a miniature dyke. This caused any amount of amusement (let me tell you, to the spectators only). Talk about Rugby. It wasn't in it. Of course, you could not handle the ball and you can guess what happened every time we descended into the pit. As a matter of fact it only required water in it to have made the heavens more than a little sultry.

Possibly the most meritorious performance of the season was the drawn game against Spilsby. This was the first time they had ever been held by the Town, and the result was satisfactory to all concerned. I should imagine the majority who read this will smile when I tell them they had one in the forwards quite equal to International form, and this in the days when such giants of the game were knocking about as Preston North End and the Corinthians. I allude to Ben Robinson. As a matter of fact this season he was selected for North versus South, and acquitted himself very well.

Another noticeable item was the appearance of the Basford Rovers; the first team from the Notts. district. They were well received, and it was the commencement of a series of matches with Notts. Clubs, which has been the means of not only causing a friendly rivalry between us and the various elevens, but also has cemented a friendship which still remains unbroken after thirty years, and long may it last, say I.

In the Lincolnshire Cup Ties Louth were beaten, and also Brigg Ancholme, but Brigg Town avenged their townsmen, and gave us the order of the knock, only to have the same operation performed on them by Spilsby quite in their old sweet way.

Although the Town were apparently a happy family the return match with Brigg caused a fly in the ointment, inasmuch as nothing short of a strike was on the carpet. It arose through a certain party taking umbrage at his brother not being selected, and refusing to play. For the vacancy a well-known fish merchant on the Pontoon was invited, but better counsels prevailed and the full team as selected appeared on the field, with the result that we made a draw, a novelty against Brigg in the old days.

After the match as usual we quite enjoyed ourselves. Any amount of chaffing was knocking about, and since then I have had many a laugh with my old friend, J.T. Barley, still in the land of the living, who made the assertion that although we might beat them at cricket we should never beat them at football. I reminded him of it when Grimsby Town were in the First Division, and also told him we could send about half a last of clubs to whack them, but he only laughed and closed the argument by inviting me to adjourn and have a wee drappie. We both agreed on this point at all events.

Grimsby Town, now well afloat, commenced season 1882-3 with any amount of confidence, for not only had they secured the ground for another season from Ike Good (the best local cricketer Grimsby ever produced), but they had received some valuable acquisition to the team, viz., the Rev. J. F. Flowers, W. King, H. Monument, G. France and S. Noble. True, the ground appointments were nothing out of the ordinary, but for the first time we enjoyed the luxury of having dressing accommodation. It consisted of two bathing vans, slightly different to that enjoyed by the present generation, but in those days we were thankful for small mercies, and it certainly was the means of our being able to keep our ordinary apparel dry at all events.

If for nothing else this season is noticeable for a better class of matches all round. For instance, besides local teams, fixtures were arranged with Notts. Forest; Sheffield Pyebank, and Lincoln Albion, the first English Cup Tie ever played at Grimsby, against Phœnix Bessemer, a team from the Rotherham district, and the formation of the Lincolnshire County team. Locally we quite held our own, beating Louth Town twice by 6–0, 6–1. Spilsby, as usual were too good for us, in fact with a full team on, they were practically in a class by themselves, so far as Lincolnshire was concerned. As a set off, however, we made a good fight with Brigg Town.

Re the Louth match. Rather an amusing incident occurred. As usual a large number of supporters journeyed with us, amongst them was a well-known smack owner, Fred O. On arriving home he crossed to the other platform, and seeing a train stationed there jumped aboard with several of his friends saying "Here's a train for the Docks." Off it went and to Fred's dismay the first stoppage was Waltham. Considering that we had come from Louth by the last train, this was a bit rough. However, they decided to go through, coming back by trap, but Fred was chaffed many a day on the pontoon about this little incident. On the eve of the first English Cup Tie there was naturally any amount of excitement. Phœnix Bessemer were an unknown club as far as their abilities were concerned, and not a few of our supporters were of opinion that at least we should make a good fight of it. Therefore imagine their dismay when we were literally run off our feet. Yes, there is no getting away from the fact. They were all over us, and I for one was very glad when the whistle blew. True, the score, nine goals to one, was not a true criterion of the run of the game, but the form shown by them was distinctly superior to anything hitherto seen in the Fisheries.

In the Lincolnshire Cup we were destined to make a far better show. In fact for the first time we reached the semi-final, only to be knocked out by Brigg Town, who, as usual, underwent the same operation at the feet of Spilsby. After beating Brigg Britannia in the first round by 2 goals to 1, we were drawn against a supposed cheap thing, viz., the M. S. and L. Steamship Department, commonly known as the Ironsides. Being a local team any amount of interest was taken in it, despite our supposed superiority. A large crowd assembled, and to everybody's surprise, including our own, they made the pace a cracker, and six minutes from time were actually losing by one goal to nil. Then when a win seemed a dead cert. for them, we scored, and a minute from time added the winning goal.

The latter was one of the most remarkable I ever saw. Fred Marshall was so tired that he was sat down in the field of play, not off-side of course, but the ball coming his way he jumped up and to our delight scored as fine a goal as ever you saw. The Ironsides were terribly disappointed, as, truth to tell, on the play they deserved to win, but like good sportsmen they took their defeat very well, and the captain was one of the first to congratulate us on our success.

Since that date Tom Atkinson and I have had many a laugh over a little incident which occurred on the eve of the match. Having to complete arrangements for the ground, several of us went to Tom's house to interview him. On arriving outside we heard Tom's voice, and to our surprise he was lecturing them on the beauties of the short passing game, with the assistance of the blackboard, one similar to those used in any ordinary Board School. We ridiculed it at the time, but it was only by a rare stroke of luck that it was not the means of relieving Grimsby Town of any further anxiety re the destination of the Cup for that season. The following were the teams :—

GRIMSBY TOWN.

Goal, Rev. J. F. Flowers.
Backs, J. Warner and A. Ousey.
Half-backs, R. C. Hall and R. Lincoln.
Right wing, H. Monument and S. Noble.
Centres, F. Marshall and G. France.
Left wing, F. Lowe and A. H. Read.

S.S. DEPARTMENT.

Goal, G. Atkinson.

Backs, W. King and G. Kimpson.

Half-backs, T. Leonard, T. Atkinson and H. Watson.

Right wing, H. Atkinson and W. Frith.

Centre, H. Hyde.

Left wing, J. Brelsford and C. Atkinson.

A casual glance will enable those who wade through the column to perceive that the teams were differently arranged in the half-back line, the Ironclads playing three half-backs and sacrificing a forward. Tom claims this was the first time this was done in this district, but he is scarcely correct as both the Wanderers and White Star had done it, but all the same it was a distinct success, and it certainly was very strange that it was years after before it was generally adopted by the leading clubs.

In the next round we had the luxury of a bye, but in the semi-final had the bad luck to be drawn against Brigg Town at Brigg, and after a desperate struggle were defeated by three goals to nil. Something like a thousand spectators journeyed by the specials. The excitement was tremendous, and only those who visited Brigg in the old days have any idea of the partizanship shown by the home spectators, who were firm believers in the win, tie or wrangle business. This was one of the occasions when a bodyguard had to be provided for the goalkeeper. Yes, Harry certainly had a lively time of it. Considering this was the first time we had reached the Semi-Final perhaps it may be as well to give the teams. Here they are :—

GRIMSBY TOWN.

Goal, H. Evans.

Backs, Flowers and Warner.

Half-backs, Read and Hall.

Right wing, Lowe and Monument.

Centres, Lincoln and Brown.

Left wing, Noble and France.

BRIGG TOWN.

Goal, H. Rose.

Backs, Barley and J. Rowbottom.

Half-backs, Storm, Bartle and Walker.

Right wing, Hett and Wood.

Centre, W. Rowbottom.

Left wing, E. Rose and E. Rowbottom.

After the excitement of the Cup Ties, it was a pleasure to return to the ordinary matches, and quite a jovial party made the journey to Nottingham to see us play the first match against the Forest. But what a day. I am somewhat amused at the temerity, or something else, of the Leicester Fosse team this season refusing to finish the match against the Town. They ought to have been with us. It literally came down in torrents, and certainly it was the worst day I ever turned out to play in. How they beat us seven goals to nil is a matter of history, but there is always a silver lining to every cloud, and we saw it inasmuch as we did our first bit of poaching, and induced Harry Taylor, one of their full backs, to return home with us. He was a good man and might have played much longer, if he had taken care of himself, but like not a few other good men, he was too fond of lifting his elbow, with the result that his services had to be dispensed with.

As expected Sheffield Pyebank were too good for us, but we beat Lincoln Albion at Lincoln. Well do I remember the match. It was played on the ground known as the Cow Paddle. We had goal posts if is true, but no touch line. The cows had been drifted from that particular portion, but not before leaving numerous deposits. This caused rather an amusing incident to all but the unfortunate party immediately concerned, as one of our team had the misfortune to be tripped, and glided head first through one of the aforesaid deposits. This was something like a foul was it not?

With the formation of Lincolnshire County, the one topic of conversation was how many of the Town team would be selected. In the first match against Hallamshire (Sheffield District), Flowers and Hall were the only two, but in several of the other matches Harry Monument came on the scene. All of them deserved their positions, Flowers for his judgment and tackling, Hall for his throwing in alone, whilst Monument was one of the best dribblers in the County, very fast on the ball and took some stopping. To some of the rising generation it may appear somewhat paradoxical for a footballer to be good enough for a team through his throwing abilities alone, but for their edification it may be just as well to state that the throw in in the old days was vastly different to that of the present day, whereas the present one scarcely

ESTABLISHED 1876.

C. SHEPHARD & SON,

The Swag Shop,

170, FREEMAN STREET,

GRIMSBY.

Brush Manufacturers,

WHOLESALE AND RETAIL.

Glass, China, Smallware, and General Merchants.

Shops and Hawkers supplied at Lowest Possible Prices.

PAPER BAGS, BREAD PAPER, TWINE, &c.

Shephard's $4\frac{1}{2}$d. Bazaar,

162, FREEMAN STREET.

Useful and Fancy Articles, Toys, Paints, &c.

penalises the opponents the old one was practically as good as a penalty if Charlie took it in our opponents' half. The goal keepers dreaded it, and not without cause as invariably with one hand he landed it bang into goal, and with six forwards closing in, the man between the sticks had quite a lively time. What do you think?

This season some people had an idea that there was little difference between the Town and the other local team, the White Star. Considering we never met it was difficult to draw the line, but without showing any bias, I honestly believe the Town was the better team of the two. True, they beat Hull Town three goals to one, a good performance, but they came an awful cropper when they met Brigg, losing by eight goals to nil. Singular to relate, this occurred on the same date as Phœnix Bessemer were putting us through it. So things in general were pretty lively from a Grimbarian-point of view. For the sake of reference I append the team that invariably played for the White Star this season—

Goal, C. Thompson.
Backs, W. King and G. Kimpson.
Half-backs, J. Corden, J. Forman and W. Earle.
Right wing, J. Ellis (captain) and J. Earle.
Centre, W. Balch.
Left wing, R. Fanthorpe and G. Heyhoe.

Financially! As may be expected our treasury was not over-burdened with the all necessary. However, notwithstanding that a large amount of prejudice existed amongst the general public against the game, it is satisfactory to note that, thanks to the players being strictly amateurs, the termination of the season found the club with a balance in hand, a novelty, even in the old days.

After last season's success the Committee looked forward with every confidence to the future, and a capital list of fixtures was arranged, including matches with Notts. Forest, Sheffield Pyebank, Manchester Greenheys, Spilsby, Gainsborough Trinity, Brigg Town, Hull Town, &c., whilst fixtures were arranged for the Town Wanderers with M. S. and L. Department, Brigg Town and Hull Town Seconds, Hull Marlborough, Humber Rovers, &c. After all, the most noteworthy item was the arrangement made with Mr. Hill to play the whole of the fixtures on the Clee Park Gardens. True, at this period sports and running handicaps were occasionally held there, but on the days when matches were played the Town had the exclusive use of the grounds. This naturally was a great advantage, as not only had they for the first time in their career capital accommodation for dressing by utilising the old dancing saloon, but they likewise were enabled to have a ground thoroughly equipped in conformity to the rules of the Football Association. Also, having the ground properly enclosed, were enabled to charge for admission. Without going into the question of terms, it is satisfactory to note that they were by no means excessive, one of them being that the Town Club played a match against Manchester Greenheys, a team new to the Fisheries, on Good Friday, Mr. H. taking the whole of the gate, and, as an equivalent, paying the train fare and giving a tea to both teams, &c. The proprietor likewise arranged another novelty, viz., the first six-a-side contest ever played, also some sports, the result being that his benefit was a success in every sense of the word.

With Tom Atkinson as captain their prospects were of the brightest. They more than held their own against local teams, Brigg Town being defeated quite early on. As usual they took it very badly, in fact they disputed the decisions of both umpires. In those days a referee was not always appointed, and this happened to be one of them. I think, however, speaking from memory, this was about the last occasion, and quite right, too, as it was quite necessary that one should be appointed to decide between the rival umpires, who, I am afraid, occasionally showed more than a little partizanship for their respective sides.

This season it was decided to make a determined effort to make a good show in both the Lincoinshire and English Cup Ties. Having been drawn against Hull Town in the first round of the National Trophy, as a preliminary canter it was decided to arrange a match with Spilsby on neutral ground, Louth being selected. The negotiations were successful, and once more we met our antagonists. A good crowd went with our team, only to see us defeated once more. It is satisfactory to note, however, the margin was only one goal, but this was thought to be quite good enough for Hull Town, and so it proved, as they were defeated somewhat easily, to the delight of a large number of supporters, who, journeyed with the team.

In the second round, however, we came an awful cropper at Grantham, losing by four goals to nil. I well remember the day. After a veritable blizzard the snow laid about four inches on the ground, and the home team being much the heavier and better shod, literally left our team standing. Still it was a terrible disappointment, but in the old days we knew how to enjoy ourselves, and you can take it that it was a jovial crowd that journeyed home that night.

Notwithstanding their early dismissal in the National Competition, any amount of confidence was felt that the time had arrived when we should either lift the Lincolnshire Cup or, at all events, make a better show than we usually did. With Tom Atkinson as captain, not only did the team go in for systematic training, but players' meetings were held, and the various points concerning the game were discussed. In the preliminary rounds our opponents were easily beaten. with the result that we were drawn against Gainsborough Trinity away from home. Never before in the history of the game had there been so much excitement. Quite 1,000 supporters journeyed by the two excursions. We were met by a band, who played the team on to the ground, and to the delight of all the Town won somewhat easily by four goals to one. On arriving home another band was waiting, and quite a triumphant procession was held, which was surely a little premature considering that it was only the semi-final.

One incident occurred in connection with this semi-final, which had a direct bearing on the future of the club from a financial point of view. For some time Debus and Whitehead had run excursions occasionally when the Town had an important Cup Tie away from home, and a few of us on the committee thought it would be just as well if we took the risk by giving a guarantee to the Company, and ran the excursion on behalf of the club. At our meeting, which was always held on the Monday night, we duly made the application. To our surprise Debus and Whitehead had got theirs in on the Saturday. This was rather awkward, but the Committee of Grimsby Town were not easily beaten in the old days. A committee meeting was at once summoned, and although the match was arranged for the Saturday and the bills were out we determined not to be bluffed, and got over the difficulty by postponing the match. This was kept dark for a day or two, but Mr. Judson, the station-master, being a very decent sort of fellow, we decided to acquaint him with the fact ere it was divulged to the general public. With this object in view, a few of us waited upon him. You ought to have seen his surprise. For some time he thought we were joking, but a wire soon convinced him otherwise, and the excursion organised by Messrs. Debus and Whitehead was cancelled. Perhaps ours was rather a drastic policy to adopt, but considering that we received no less than £15 1s. 2d. commission on the two excursions run to Gainsborough and Brigg, you will agree with me that the policy was quite justified by results.

Although it is no less than twenty-eight years since, it is very certain, with possibly the exception of the excursions to Bradford last year in the English Cup Tie, there has never been so many people journey with the team as went to Brigg to see the Town play Spilsby for the final. For weeks it had been the topic of conversation, the general opinion being that at length Grimsby would lift the Cup. Something approaching three thousand left the Fisheries on that day, and literally took possession of Brigg. Clearly it was a red letter day for the little town, as the visitors did not usually journey without the all necessary, and what is more to the point, were not frightened of parting with it. Re the game, after a desperate struggle, during which Grimsby Town once got in front, Spilsby for the third time in succession won the cup, and truth to tell on their merits, too.

Although defeated once more, the enthusiasm of the supporters increased rather than otherwise. Indeed, at this period of the game, it was nothing unusual for a skipper to refuse to go to sea on the eve of a match, and they also generally managed to arrive in dock the day before, or on the morning of an important match.

In the glamour of the Cup Ties we are liable to forget that there was another important club in the Fisheries stronger than ever they have been. I allude to the Grimsby and District Club. Since last season the White Star had merged into them. Naturally this strengthened the team. Joe Mason joined them as captain, and with Raynes and Hopewell they quite held their own locally, in fact Spilsby only beat them one to nil. True, this was at Grimsby, but all the same it was a fine performance.

When Billy Hopewell first appeared for the Grimsby and District Club few people imagined he was destined to become one of the best local lads ever brought out, also the first professional Middlesbrough Ironopolis ever had, but it is nevertheless a fact. He was very smart indeed, but his play was marred by a trick which although clever, was certainly not fair. It consisted in throwing one leg out, in fact, practically kneeling down. Of course his opponent being taken unawares, invariably came down a cropper. This caused rather a lively incident at the Trent Bridge. I was on the line when we were playing Notts. County. At this period Billy Gunn, the International footballer and cricketer, was in his prime, and it was a sight for the gods to see him sail down the wing. As usual, Billy waited for him. Gunn, having heard of the trick, evaded him. Always a gentleman, either on the field or off, at half-time he took Hopewell on one side, and gave him some good advice, telling him it would have been the easiest thing in the world for him to have crippled him for life by dropping on it, and he hoped for the future he would discontinue the trick. Unfortunately Billy ignored his advice, and years after the very thing very nearly occurred that Gunn predicted.

At this period without saying that we had adopted it, there is no doubt there was a certain amount of veiled professionalism knocking about, and the Football Association, instead of endeavouring to crush it, offered the Olive Branch. Naturally the clubs thought it was a tree and took it as such, so it became more prevalent than ever. Briefly, the rule passed by the Football Association was as follows :— A player is allowed to always receive his expenses, and one day's pay per week, incurred through absence from work caused by footballing, but he must in all cases furnish a written receipt, which must be produced in case of an enquiry. This, it is thought, will prevent football from becoming a profession, but at the same time will allow those desirous of playing to do so without the loss of a day's pay, which, in the case of a working man, is a great consideration. I should imagine the above is quite enough to make the present day followers of the game produce his best double-six smile.

How to evade this rule was clearly not a very difficult matter, one of the favourite methods being to work it through the wage list of any employer, who happened to employ them. For instance, if Mr. D—— plumber, for the sake of argument, required a labourer, Tom Jones was engaged, say, at a salary of twenty-five shillings a week. Perhaps the said player got tired. This unfortunately was a common practice among some — but still he got the full amount of time in by some miraculous means, and got his full wages. Yes, the time sheet was all solid, also the employer, the latter having the deficiency made up on the quiet.

After the capital season enjoyed by the Town Club, the supporters thought it quite opportune to organise a good dinner. Personally, I must acknowledge I saw no objection to the scheme, neither did anyone else in command, the result was that the Masonic Hall was engaged, and the first annual dinner of the Grimsby Town Football Club held. The leading lights of the Town were present. The very name of Levi Heyhoe should be quite sufficient to guarantee that the toys supplied were of the best, and, you can take my tip, they were freely sampled. If for nothing else, this dinner was the means of causing additional interest to be taken in the welfare of the Club, a not surprising result, as, when the evening advanced the participants swore, by all the gods and otherwise, that a team should be got together to lift that blessed Lincolnshire Cup, and also that a grand stand should be erected in Clee Park Gardens.

Within a few weeks, the all necessary having been subscribed, tenders were invited for the erection of the stand, the present Alderman Smethurst advancing the all necessary. Mr. Marrows secured the contract, and it is interesting to note that Jack Taylor was one of the joiners to erect the same. Whether the atmosphere was more salubrious than Spilsby I am not aware, but for sometime Jack had been the means more than a little of preventing us from lifting the Cup, and it was thought it might be just as well if he wore the colours of Grimsby Town in the future.

How he served the Town for quite a number of years, bar a short interval when he migrated up north, will be referred to later on, but to a certainty his arrival in the Fisheries was never regretted by any of the persons concerned. Re the stand. It accommodated about five hundred spectators, and was a paying concern from the first. True, it was rather primitive in comparison to those, say of the present day, but it was much appreciated and answered our purpose for quite a number of years.

Possibly a few remarks re the balance-sheet for season 1883-4 may be interesting. At the annual general meeting held at Dring's, for the election of officers, it was duly produced. The receipts apparently were £53 14s. 11d., and we finished up with £15 14s. 5d. in hand. Considering that we gave a donation of £10 10s. to the Grimsby Hospital, it is very evident that at this period we were not overburdened with veiled professionalism.

For the first time the Club adopted colours for the team, and very attractive they looked, having a tendency to give them quite a massive appearance.

They were royal blue and cardinal jerseys with Borough Arms on breast, white knickers, blue cap and cardinal hose.

With an attractive programme it cannot be said that the charges for admission were excessive. Here they are :— Members 5s., tickets for enclosure and grand stand 2s. 6d., ladies' season ticket, including grand stand, 5s.

Perhaps the only fly in the ointment was that Tom Atkinson, the captain for last season, absolutely refused to take it on. This caused considerable comment at the time, the majority of the public having the idea that friction existed between the Club and Tom, but it was nothing of the kind. He simply wished to remain loyal to the Ironclads, a team he founded, and which, without his tuition and captainship on the field, was like a ship without a rudder. The result was. that R. C. Hull was selected to fill the vacancy. Never a more popular man donned the colours, but it would be absurd to think he possessed the judgment of his predecessor, and to an extent the team suffered in consequence.

Ever progressive, the Committee of Grimsby Town, not content with the usual local football, were determined to test their strength against the cream of the talent, and no less a team than Blackburn Olympic were induced to visit Clee Park. In 1883 and 4, they had accomplished what every team of note in the North had been trying to do for a number of years, but only after a desperate struggle, as they played extra time ere they defeated the Old Etonians, and won the English Cup. Well, they duly arrived, and a good crowd assembled, only to see the visitors rub it in to some tune, inasmuch as they helped themselves to nine goals. How they obtained them is a matter of history. They literally played with our lot, but the lesson was not lost, as more than one wrinkle was picked up by the home team.

It perhaps may be interesting to note that when Blackburn Olympic won the Cup we had no "Sunday Chronicle," no, nor Brook's telegrams; in fact only a few of us were interested enough to meet the first train on the Monday morning to see the result in the "Nottingham Guardian."

Locally the team had a capital year, beating Spilsby somewhat easily, in fact they had an unbeaten record as far as Lincolnshire was concerned, bar the Cup-tie with Gainsborough Trinity. In the remaining matches they more than held their own. Not bad, considering they met clubs of the calibre of Blackburn Olympic, Notts Forest, Sheffield Pyebank, Sneinton Institute, Notts.

Olympic, Mellers Limited, Long Eaton Rangers, &c. Personally I have nothing but pleasant recollections of the majority of these matches, as it was invariably the custom to adjourn to Dring's Hotel and have tea. Not at all a bad idea, what do you think?

There have been so many yarns knocking about *re* the refereeing of your humble servant that perhaps a word or two may not be out of place. It used to be quite a common saying when I entered the field in command of the whistle, "We're all right, the Town will win today," but I can conscientiously say that I never gave a wrong decision wilfully. True, some of my decisions may have appeared surprising to some of the spectators surrounding the field of play, but invariably they consisted of individuals either blinded by partizanship, or their idea of the rules were crude in the extreme.

On one occasion I caught it particularly warm. One of the Notts. teams was playing, and through a late kick off there was a danger of them missing their train. During the second half their Umpire came to me and asked if it was possible to play ten minutes short. After consulting our official I agreed. Unfortunately for me they happened to lead when the period arrived. Of course, I blew the whistle, and knew about it afterwards, but then we lost you know. It might have been slightly different had it been otherwise.

A rather amusing incident occurred shortly after. Whether the Umpire belonging to the opposing side had heard a whisper *re* my refereeing I am not aware, but it leaked out that he was going to keep an eye on me, especially regarding the time. He was one of those fussy little individuals with an idea of his own, and R. C. Hall, who was umpiring this day, and myself determined to have a lark with him. With this object in view it was arranged that I should be continually asking him the right time in the second half. Eventually it had the desired effect. He came across and asked me if I had a watch. At that time I wore a double chain, and not receiving an answer he asked to look at it. I said "Help yourself." Imagine his surprise when he found one pocket occupied by a beer barrel key and the other by a watch entirely devoid of hands. Of course, I had arranged with Charlie to give me the tip when time was up, so the incident passed unnoticed by the crowd.

Possibly the roughest experience I ever had was in a Cup-tie at Brigg, between the Town team and Spilsby. By some means or other the Referee from Sheffield missed his train, with the result that the officials of both teams waited upon me and asked me to take charge of the whistle. At first I refused, but ultimately I consented, and a lively time I had. Spilsby had much the better of the game and won easily. I can conscientiously say I refereed to the best of my ability, and gave no unfair decisions, but a section of the home spectators thought differently, and at the termination of the game, when I stepped under the ropes, one of them landed me a beauty. Not being a believer in the old maxim of a kiss for a blow I retaliated, and luckily for myself in particular, "Cob" and the usual crowd were near, and eventually, with the assistance of the police, we fought our way out of the field. Naturally I came off the worst. Whether they took me for a football or not is an open question, but they booted me pretty freely with the result that I could scarcely walk. Luckily for me the Spilsby team had engaged a drag to convey them to Elsham Station, and they invited me in. Immediately I stepped in the Driver recognising me, said "Halloo, here's the sanguinary referee," and endeavoured to slash me with the whip, but the blow never descended. As a matter of fact, he did, as Billy Shaw, one of the team, who was on the box with him, knocked him clean off it, and whipping the reins up, speedily had us at the station.

Naturally the greatest interest was centred in the Cup Ties, and a strong feeling was prevalent that the time had at length arrived when the Lincolnshire Cup would find a place on our President's sideboard, but once more we were disappointed as, after beating the Ironclads, Barton and Louth, we received our quietus from Gainsborough Trinity. I well remember the match. As usual the excursions were crowded. The greatest excitement prevailed, and when A. H. Read had his collar bone broken it was only the presence of the police that prevented a miniature riot. It is not my intention to make any excuses for the Town team, but to a certainty this was one of the roughest matches ever seen in the fen district, and whatever the Referee was doing to allow Brown to continue his tactics and remain on the field was the subject of comment for many a long day. However, it is satisfactory to note that Grantham, a much heavier team, played a similar game in the final, and beat them after a terrible struggle and the Cup by way of a change adorned Mr. Hutchinson's sideboard, a brother, by the way, of the late Canon Hutchinson.

It was rather a singular coincidence that we should figure in the fourth round in both competitions, but the fact is nevertheless there, and for the first time on record the Town figured in the fourth round of the English Cup. Of course, there was no comparison in the calibre of the competitors the Town met. For instance, in the first round the future holders of the Lincolnshire Cup, Grantham, were met, and they were only defeated after a drawn game. Redcar, being induced to play the second round in the Fisheries suffered the same fate, whilst the third round found us drawn against our dear friends, Lincoln City, who also received the order of the knock. After this we naturally got amongst the big fishers, being drawn away against the Old Carthusians. Just by way of a change, I was not present at the match, for the very good and sufficient reason that I was getting married at the time, but without beating about the bush it was very evident that our team were outclassed. This is not very surprising considering they had amongst their players men of the calibre of Cobbold, the future International, and probably one of the hardest shots for goal that ever played, if not the hardest. If we got beaten, the usual crowd enjoyed themselves thoroughly, one in particular will not forget it in a hurry, as he got chaffed for many a day about a little incident that occurred on the field of play. It happened thus. The majority of the spectators being swells, naturally donned the long hat, and were persistently calling out, "Well played, Charterhouse." One of our crowd, to the amusement of all around, after enquiring after the names, at length called out, "Where the capital H is he?" Of course Charterhouse is the name of the College from which the team took the name of Old Carthusians.

It will be noticed in this competition that Redcar were induced to play their Cup Tie in the Fisheries, a novelty, in those days of course. It was the first time it had ever occurred in this district, and although they probably shared a better gate, the sole reason which caused them to waive their choice of ground, it was a doubtful policy, as they were not half a bad team, and might easily have beaten us if we had journeyed up North.

Another item, which may surprise a few is the fact that on November 22nd, no less than three elevens, with the necessary officials, were placed on the field, viz., Grimsby Town, Grimsby Town Wanderers, and the Grirnsby Town Colts. What is more satisfactory is that they won all the matches, a very smart performance, considering that their opponents were Sheffield Pyebank, Brigg Ancholme and Cleethorpes.

On the termination of the Cup Ties, the interest was naturally centred in the match with Manchester Greenheys as per arrangement with Mr. Hill, and as an additional attraction, the programme included a six-a-side contest, with sports afterwards. This caused a tremendous crowd to gather round the enclosure, at least six thousand paying at the gate, clearly a record. After the Town had beaten the Greenheys by four goals to nil, a very satisfactory and also surprising result, the ground was cleared for the six-a-side contest A capital entry had been secured, the clubs competing being as follows :— Pike Noble's team, Gainsborough Trinity, Grimsby Town, Men of Harlech (H. Evans' team, but really the second team of the Town), Ironsides, Lincoln City, Barton Town, Brigg Town, Manchester Greenheys, Sheffield and Notts. Forest. After a capital contest Sheffield won the gold medals, and Lincoln City the silver as runners up. It cannot be denied that the best team won. Indeed when the names are analysed it would have been surprising if they had not. Here they are :— Gregory, Brayshay (who afterwards kept the pub now known as the Empire, in Victoria Street and played for Grimsby Town), Moss, Mosforth, Winterbottom, and Frank Hoole. One at least, Mosforth, was an international, and possibly the best dribbler of the day, whilst the other four repeatedly played for Sheffield against Glasgow, etc., matches looked upon as second only to the Internationals, whilst Frank Hoole was no other than the well-known fish merchant on the pontoon. I should like to see that medal, Frank.

For the information of those who have never seen a six-a-side contest, they can take it from me the players wanted to be hot stuff. It was absolutely imperative that they were not only in the pink of condition, but likewise something out of the ordinary on the ball, as it frequently occurred that one individual practically took it the whole length of the ground to notch a goal for his side.

This season the Grimsby and District early on had the idea that they were quite on a par with the Town. True, with Joe Mason as captain, and other fresh arrivals, they did not make a bad show, but truth to tell, it was the old story. Lack of the almighty dollar prevented extra talent, shall I say, being induced to play for them, and the consequence was that signs were not wanting that the Town Club was gradually forging ahead, in fact, they were firmly established as the leading club in this district, if not in the County.

For some time a dispute had been raging between the White Star, now the Grimsby and District, and the Ironclads, as to the destination of the cup, given by Mr. Hill in the Clee Park Gardens last season. The White Star claimed they had won it outright, whereas the Ironclads said it had to be won three times in succession. To settle the dispute a capital suggestion was made by Mr. Willmer, to the effect that it should be put up for competition amongst junior clubs for the benefit of the Grimsby and District Hospital. The idea was adopted, and the result was that after a spirited competition the Perseverance became the first holders of the Cup, beating the Humber Rovers in the final.

Although the ordinary season was supposed to finish at the end of April there was no recognised close season, therefore not only did the junior teams continue playing practically throughout the summer, but thanks to the success of the six-a-side contests on the Good Friday, others were arranged, the second tournament terminating in favour of the local team, consisting of J. H. Taylor, H. Taylor, G. H. Home (an Accrington player), W. Hopewell, H. Atkinson, and S. Norman (Nottingham). Some idea of the interest taken in these contests can be formed by the number of entries, viz., eighteen for the first division, and no less than thirty-four for the minor contest.

At the annual general meeting harmony prevailed, and after the balance-sheet had been passed, a very important suggestion was made, viz., that a financial secretary be appointed, and Mr. I. J. P. was selected. To the casual follower of the game perhaps little importance was attached to this office, but they can take it from me that it was a move in the right direction, and highly necessary for the welfare of the Club, as just now we were commencing to have a much increased turnover from a financial point of view, and it was infinitely better to have this section of the club worked by a small committee.

W. T. Lammin once more consented to figure as the secretary, and his services were invaluable. With some, perhaps, the idea may be prevalent that in the old days the office was a mere sinecure, but I can assure them they can disabuse their minds of this idea, and the present generation have much to thank the late W. T. L. for. With G. Kimpson as captain and J. H. Taylor as vice, everything promised well for the ensuing season, and so it turned out, as it was destined to be the best in the history of the club. With the capital list of matches arranged, the newcomers being Horncastle, Leeds (so you see they had a club 25 years ago), Sheffield Attercliffe, and Park Grange, Derby St. Lukes, Rawtenstall, etc., and the promise of something exciting both in the English and County Cup Ties, there was any amount of enthusiasm knocking about, and this journey it was decided to hold the annual dinner in the Town Hall. Considering I have frequently been asked where this dinner was held, I append a copy of the card. Here it is :—

GRIMSBY TOWN FOOTBALL CLUB.

Established 1878.

ANNUAL DINNER.

Held at the Town Hall, Great Grimsby, September 9th, 1885.

Chairman: Councillor H. Smethurst.

Vice-Chairman: Mr. C. F. Carter.

TOAST LIST.

"Queen," Chairman.

"Prince and Princess of Wales and Family," Chairman.

"Army, Navy and Volunteers," proposed by Mr. A. Baker, responded to by Captain A. Bannister.

"Mayor and Corporation," proposed by, Mr. R. Mason, responded to by the Mayor, Councillor C. Morton.

"Town and Trade," proposed by Mr. F. Osborn, responded to by Mr. A. Green.

"Success to the Grimsby Town Football Club," proposed by Mr. R. Lincoln, responded to by Mr. G. Kimpson.

"Hon. Members," proposed by Mr. W. J. Webster, responded to by Mr. W. G. Marshall.

"Officers of Club," proposed by Mr. H. S. Mundahl, responded to by Vice-chairman.

"Other Clubs," proposed by Mr. J. Shepherd, responded to by Mr. Willmer.

"The Press," proposed by Mr. F. Barrett, responded to by Members of Press.

"Chairman and Vice-chairman," proposed by Mr. A. Burnham, responded to by Chairman and Vice-Chairman.

"Ladies," proposed by Mr. G. Atkinson, responded to by Mr. T. Lundie.

From the above it is very evident that it was quite a representative gathering, jovial, and yet of a quite business character. Among other items Mr. C. F. C. made the statement that the average amount of fish sent daily by rail was two hundred tons, but one day last week no less than 600 tons was sent — a record. He qualified it by making a statement to the effect that it was impossible to imagine how much the fishing industry would develop. Evidently Mr. C. F. C. knew something.

With the strong list of fixtures it was very necessary that the team should be strengthened, and Jack Seal and Dick Sharman were secured. Later on in the season Harry Smith, commonly known as "Cobbold," joined the team, but I well remember the difficulty a few of us had in getting him a trial. There is an old saying, "A prophet is no good in his own country," and this applies to this day to local talent in the football world. It is astonishing the prejudice that exists against a local man, and so it was with Harry, but he speedily justified his selection, and was a tower of strength to the Club for many years. It cannot be said by any stretch of the imagination that he was an attractive player, but perhaps he gave his best definition of his abilities to a Notts. County player. I well remember it. After the match, one of the Notts. team was in common vernacular trying to get a rise out of him, and said he could never play in his life. "No," Cob said, "perhaps not, but I can stop a — capital H, Mr. Printer — of you — also capital B — that think you can."

Locally, and otherwise, in the friendly matches, the Town had a grand season, but it was in the Cup Ties where the excitement prevailed, and Grimsby Town clearly established a record, perhaps of a doubtful character, never before or since. It consisted of being on the carpet before the Football Association both for the English and Lincolnshire County Competitions. The former perhaps was of a rather trivial nature, but the latter was something out of the ordinary, and I will endeavour later on to give a brief outline of the most sensational protest ever before the Football Association.

Giving the English Cup the preference, fate ordained that we should meet our dear friends the Cits, and just by way of a change we relieved them of any further anxiety re the distinction of the English Cup. Perhaps the operation was somewhat annoying to Mr. J. H. S. and crowd, but I can assure you in this locality the sympathy towards them was conspicuous by its absence. Darlington were our next victims, and our lads piled the agony on to some tune, no less than eight goals being scored against the Quakers. Then came the tug of war. The luck of the game caused us to be drawn against Middlesbrough away from home, and it was known that the chances were against us, but it was only after a desperate struggle that they beat us two to one. Indeed, the chances are that if Harry Monument had not been taken ill when we arrived we might at least have made a draw of it. But after all, this is the luck of the game. Re the carpet business, concerning the Middlesbrough match. It was of quite a trivial character. The day previous to the match there had been a heavy fall of snow, and the ground was covered inches deep. The consequences was that it was mutually agreed to postpone the match, but unfortunately the parent Association were not notified to that effect. Hence the fly in the ointment. However, they did not take a serious view of it, and the fixture duly came off.

Little did we think when we embarked on the voyage to capture the county cup, that it would lead to the most sensational protest ever dealt with by the Football Association, and ere the year was over proof was not wanting that amongst other items it was an undisguised blessing that we not only had a smart committee and officials at the helm, but likewise had adopted the policy of having a small committee to work the financial part of the business.

In the early ties we had little difficulty, even when we ran against the holders of the county trophy, Grantham Town, but when we met Lincoln City there was every appearance of a great struggle, as we were drawn to play within the shadow of Big Tom. Truth to tell, a bitter feeling existed between both the players and the executive of both teams, and clearly it had not been lessened by the whacking the Cits got in the English Cup. Briefly speaking, although rough, it was an even game and at the termination of time the Cits wanted to play the extra half-hour, and of course we declined, and left the field. Naturally we expected to replay it at Clee Park, but to our surprise received a notification from the English Association that we had been reported for not playing the extra time. Then the fun began. The Secretary of the County Association must have held a brief for Ananias. He swore blankly that our Umpire agreed to play extra time. Of course, he denied the soft impeachment, and the result was that although the English Association offered to arbitrate, meetings were held, and the Cits refusing to play at Clee Park, we were awarded the Tie, and ordered to play Lincoln Lindum in the Final. This we did, and after a good match, beat them two to nil, and naturally thought we had won the cup.

But, alas, we had not even got hold of the handles. Oh, dear no. Apparently we were chasing a phantom. Other meetings were held. Talk about being warm. Imagine about forty present, about evenly divided, nothing personal, not at all, simply a little friendly criticism, don't you know. As a matter of fact this is where our Finance Committee came in. Yes, there is no disguising the Cits professed to hold a little of the all necessary, and so did we, and the result hung in the balance although we always felt that we should eventually once more come off triumphant in the Committee Room. Eventually we were ordered to replay the Cup Tie at Grantham. It duly came off, and the Lincoln Lindum finished second once more.

Great was the jubilation in the fisheries, but still the Cup was not handed over, not exactly, and many an anxious hour was spent ere it landed in the Fisheries. As a matter of fact, yet another meeting was held at Lincoln, when Mr. Mundahl proposed that the Cup be presented to Grimsby Town as rightful winners of the same. Mr. Hutchinson, of Grantham, proposed as an amendment that in consequence of the present state of affairs, the Cup be held over at present, and be presented at the next General Meeting of the Association, which was carried by 19 votes to 18. Keen, wasn't it? At the same meeting it was decided to award Grimsby Town and Lincola Lindum twelve pounds each for their expenses in the first final tie. Not an excessive amount, but perhaps sufficient, as even veiled professionalism had not gained a firm foothold in the Fisheries.

If for nothing else I shall always remember the above protest for the enjoyable outing we had when we appeared before the Football Association at Kennington Oval. Then, as now, the Association always contrived to hold its meetings either at some fashionable watering place in the Summer time or in some large city where something above the average was on the boards. This journey it happened to be Oxford and Cambridge Boat Race and the final tie at Kennington Oval. Not bad, was it? Well the day duly arrived and three of us, the Secretary, a certain gentleman, and self, duly landed in the City at 6 a.m. Imagine your humble servant landing there after a six hours' journey. Well, I suggested adjourning to the St. Pancras Hotel. We did. The hour being somewhat inconvenient the waiter apologised, but consented to oblige us to the best of his ability. The first course arrived, causing me to remark, "Halloa, where did you get these sticklebacks." Much astonished he gave them quite another name. However, to be brief, I relieved him of any further anxiety as far as I was concerned by simply asking him to convey a chine of beef as carefully as he could from the adjacent sideboard, and I guaranteed to give him an exhibition. He smiled, and so did I when it arrived, what do you think?

Afterwards our friend invited us to be his guest, and after certain business had been done we accompanied him to one of the wharves, where we had a capital view of the race. Possibly, however, one of the most agreeable features of the proceedings was the appearance of the Toys, likewise the Kali, I don't think. Yes, we were having a good time, and inwardly I blessed my dear friend, Mr. J. H. S., of City fame, for being the means of causing me to have quite a red letter day in the annals of my life.

A rush from there in a cab, and what a change. On arriving at Kennington Oval where we had seats reserved, the ground was densely packed. West Bromwich were playing Blackburn Rovers, and the latter had only to win it this time to win it outright. To be brief, if ever a team ought to have won it was the Throstles. Bassett in the wing was a perfect terror, and Arthur alone in goal saved the Rovers from a crushing defeat. Result: No Goals. It is a remarkable fact that whereas the Throstles wanted to play extra time, the Rovers declined, precisely the very question we were summoned to appear before the Association on after the match.

However, the spectators settled the question by crowding on the field of play, which caused us to have the greatest difficulty in reaching the Pavilion, where the meeting was held. Eventually we arrived just in time to hear the Throstles and Rovers ordered to replay at Derby. Digressing for one moment, when the replay took place the Throstles lost by two goals. Hard lines for them.

When our case was called we soon were convinced that Major Marindin, who was in the chair, was a business man. He was a model of brevity. He simply asked our Secretary a question or two and informed him that we should either have to replay the match or be reported to them, which probably meant that we should cease to exist as a club. This was very warm, but perhaps if he had heard our remarks he would have been more than a little surprised. Briefly we said we should see him, well you know where, and as a matter of fact, did not let it mar the pleasure of the evening. Oh dear, no, that was quite out of the question. Of course, we never intended to replay, neither did we. The consequence was that we thought it as well to prepare for the approaching storm due at the annual general meeting of the Football Association. Evidently it was necessary to have full sail set, and we did it in a manner little expected at headquarters. Early on at the Lincolnshire Association meeting, I hinted at the all necessary playing an important part in the matter of delegates voting, and this being so, why should not this policy be adopted once more. Granted it was a very bold one, but those at the helm in the old days were more than seven, and did not stop at trifles. Years after when we met some of the leading lights, they even laughed at it. Well, this is how the oracle was worked. We quite recognised that by some means or other we should obtain the tickets of a sufficient number of representatives of clubs to carry the meeting, and with this object in view, some lovely baskets of fish were sent to the various officials concerned. A novelty, some might say. Perhaps it was, but my dear friends, you can take my tip, it is the correct policy to feed a man well if you want a favour, and this journey it came off, for we received no less than forty tickets. It was a jovial crowd that made the journey, and arrangements had been made with a prominent fish merchant with a shop not a thousand miles from Covent Gardens, J. B. by name (I wonder how his appetite is), to meet us with a sufficient number of his friends to represent the various tickets we had obtained. It duly came off, and the trick was done. Yes, it was positively amusing to watch the faces of the opposing crowd, but eventually they accepted the inevitable with very good grace, and thus once more Grimsby Town came off triumphant, and the road was at length clear for the much coveted trophy to find a resting place in the Fisheries.

After all this, controversy it will be readily understood that the Officials and Committee had a lively time. In fact, during the season, irrespective of numerous sub-committees, principally finance, no less than 46 meetings were held. The Secretary, self and R. C. H. had a full record, but the majority were generally found in their places when required.

Taking all round the perusal of the balance-sheet was an enjoyable item. For instance, the turnover had increased enormously, the gate money alone being £639 6s. 10d., whilst the members' subscriptions were just a paltry half-crown under the £100. Against this, the amount paid to other clubs was £345 9s. 3d., a large amount, but easily understood when no less than thirty

matches were played at Clee Park. As usual a donation was voted of £15 to the Grimsby Hospital, but possibly the most satisfactory feature of the balance-sheet was that after meeting all liabilities we had a balance of £30 18s. 7d. in the bank.

Re the performances of the teams, surely they will bear inspection. Here they are :—

FIRST ELEVEN.

Matches				Goals	
Played	Won	Drawn	Lost	For	Against
38	30	6	2	118	27

THE WANDERERS.

Matches				Goals	
Played	Won	Drawn	Lost	For	Against
21	9	7	5	40	27

Of course, allowance must be made as far as the first team was concerned that by arrangement no less than 30 matches were played at home, but nevertheless it was a brilliant performance considering the calibre of the clubs met, and it says much for the defence that the highest score against them was two goals, a record, considering the number of matches played, which I should very much doubt has been equalled in the Fen Country either before or since. This season, contrary to expectations, although their performances were overshadowed by those of the premier team, the Grimsby and District Club did some capital performances. Joe Mason, in the centre, was just in his prime, in fact he attracted the attention of the County Committee, and figured with Billy Hopewell in more than one of their fixtures.

Naturally, after the last grand season the followers of the town expected something out of the ordinary in the ensuing one, but they were doomed to disappointment as, by some means or other, and although the Committee were progressive enough, and fixed with some much stronger teams for the ordinary matches, such as Blackburn Rovers, Preston North End, Halliwell, etc., the old members of the team entirely failed to produce their old form, and the new goalkeeper, Coppack by name, being a miserable failure, things in general were anything but satisfactory.

One fixture was greatly missed from the programme, viz., Hull Town, who for some time had found a great difficulty in fulfilling their programme. How and why is easily explained. In the old days there were few clubs in Yorkshire playing the Soccer Code, and with no League or Alliance they relied on Lincolnshire for the bulk of the matches. The latter clubs were, however, by no means eager to cross the water as, occasionally, they were unable to return the same night, so the Third Porters found it practically impossible to arrange a decent programme. Perhaps, after all, the one thing that killed the Soccer Code in the Third Port was the great popularity of Rugby football. It is very strong now, but I greatly doubt whether the gates are anything like so good as they were in the old days, when Hull had their ground on the Holderness Road, just the other side of the Elephant and Castle Hotel. It was nothing out of the ordinary to have ten or twelve thousand spectators. I myself have seen twenty thousand, when they met teams of the calibre of Bradford, Wakefield Trinity, &c., in the Yorkshire Cup.

Hull in those days, with Harrison as captain, and the Calverts, Herb Bell, &c., in the team, took any amount of whacking, and I for one occasionally enjoyed a visit very much, particularly at Hull Fair time, when Mr. Sutton, a well-known Lancashire brewer, used to bring a team down. Tom Bough, one of the best sportsmen Hull ever produced, invariably invited our Secretary, W.T.L., myself and a few others of the crowd to be his guests, and the after proceedings were something to be remembered, let me tell you. At that time, after the match both teams and friends adjourned to the Queen's Hotel in George Street, the headquarters of the Hull Football Club. Billy Teal was the landlord, and a rollicking time we had. What with the toys and a bowl or two of punch afterwards, the time passed all too quickly, and you can take it from me that it was a jovial crowd that accompanied Sutton's Team to Paragon Station.

This season some individuals had the temerity to run a team of lady footballers, and they applied for a match on the Clee Park, which was refused. Nothing daunted, they secured the Victoria Cricket Ground. A fair crowd assembled. It was a terrible fiasco, and the fair maidens had a lively time, as they were unmercifully chaffed by the Pontoonites. Leaving here they appeared on the Holderness Road Ground. This fixture terminated in a riot. The people demanded their money back, but the treasurer was more than seven, and when they arrived at the turnstiles, he had departed hence with no less than 170 of the best. Quite a good haul.

With the near approach of the third annual banquet, it was decided to invite the Preston North End team, then in its prime, to play an exhibition match in the afternoon, and be our guests at the banquet at the Town Hall in the evening. The team of all the talents duly appeared and gave a masterly exhibition of the game. Truth to tell, apparently they had a little up their sleeve, but still a defeat of three goals to nil was decisive enough. The question of who played has been asked me so many times that perhaps it will be quite as well if the teams are given with the officials. Here they are :—

PRESTON NORTH END,
Coal, W. C. Rose.
Backs, Howarth and Nick Ross.
Half-backs, Robertson, Holmes and Graham.
Forwards: Right wing, Gordon and Jimmy Ross.
Centre, Thompson.
Left-wing, Dewhurst and Goodall.
Umpire, J. J. Bentley.

GRIMSBY TOWN.
G. Atkinson.
H. Taylor and J. H. Taylor.
J. Seal, S. Norman, and W. Hopewell.
H. Atkinson and T. Garnham.
T. E. Chapman.
C. Atkinson and S. Pearson.
W. T. Lammin, Umpire.

Referee, Mr. H. R. Bellamy, hon. secretary, Lincolnshire Association.

It is some satisfaction to note that if we took a back seat in the playing field we were a veritable prize packet in the Banqueting-room, and to say that the Preston North End team and their officials were surprised when they entered it is quite in order. As a matter of fact, everything was up-to-date; the decorations were excellent, the toys likewise, and no less than 150 guests assembled round the festive board. Yes, Wednesday, November 24th, 1886, was indeed a red letter day in the annals of Grimsby Town. Councillor Smethurst was in the chair the early part of the evening, but unfortunately had to leave early, Anderson Bates filling the vacancy supported by C. M. Mundahl, Alford Green, Fred Osborne (vice-presidents), C. F. Carter (hon. treasurer), W. T. Lammin (hon. secretary), H. R. Bellamy (hon. secretary Lincolnshire Association), our old friend the Spilsby goalkeeper, Banks, the Preston North End team, F. Dewhurst, the one and only J. J. Bentley, the Committee of the Town Club, and numerous other friends. We had a capital programme of music, and the usual amount of gas had to be shot out by the aspirants to oratorical fame. Any amount of nice things were said about the Town Club, both Bentley and Dewhurst expressing the opinion that they were surprised at the form shown, and we were destined to make a name in the football world. All this was very true, but I should imagine they little thought that when the North End Team made their next appearance in the Fisheries they would be extended like they were in that memorable cup-tie. Talking about gas, I remember in proposing the toast of the Lincolnshire Football Association, I literally, as it were, put my foot in it by relating a few of the little incidents that occurred during the past season ere we landed the cup, but I managed to smooth it over very well, and the enthusiasm was great when the Chairman, Anderson Bates, handed the medals to the team. Need I say that just at this period the whole of the company appeared desirous to examine the cup, likewise the contents. Yes, our host was particularly busy just then. Later on, after the toasts had been gone through and the Chairman had retired the fun became fast and furious and our friends departed with the idea that the lads of this district were anything but the innocents abroad they imagined.

In ordinary matches, the team certainly did moderately, the performance against the full team of Blackburn Rovers being by far the best. The latter were strongly represented, and Grimsby Town, playing strongly, made a draw of it, one goal each. The following was the team :—

Goal, G. Atkinson.
Backs, H. H. Taylor, I. H. Taylor.
Half-backs, R. C. Hall, J. Seal and W. Hopewell.
Forwards, H. Atkinson, T. Garnham, T. E. Chapman, S. Pearson (from Gainsborough Trinity), and Monument.

Certainly the most enjoyable match, however, was the visit of Birmingham

St. George's. Really this was a team run and managed by Harry Mitchell, of Mitchell's Brewery, one of the very best of sports, and this journey they had no reason to forget their visit to the Fisheries. Quite a crowd met them on the Saturday night. They were shown round on the Sunday, amongst the items being a sail on the river, and after the match each player had about as much fish to take home with him as would stock a small shop, and arrangements were made to send afterwards a sufficient supply for the team and friends to have a fish supper. Needless to say when we visited Brum we had a lively time, and Harry Mitchell knew how to do it too.

In the English Cup Ties the teams did nothing out of the ordinary, neither was it expected, but in the Lincolnshire hopes ran high that the team would be capable of retaining possession of the Cup. The preliminary rounds ended satisfactorily enough, and as per usual we were destined to meet the City in the final at Gainsborough. Unfortunately the bitter feeling caused by last year's dispute was still rampant, and everything pointed to a terrific struggle. And so it proved. Up to ten minutes to time Grimsby led by one. George, just by way of a change, made a blunder, and, hey presto, the City had equalised. This journey nothing was said about extra time, and it was arranged to play it off on the same ground a fortnight hence. With the best of intentions our Committee decided to put the eleven in strict training. The headquarters were at Dring's Hotel, the whole of the team being accommodated, but, strange to say, although they had the best of everything, when the eventful day arrived they were distinctly stale, and if the Town had been represented by marionettes the City could not have had an easier task to land the County Cup for the first time. Personally then, as now, I was against training of this description, but possibly what had more than a little to do with the improved play of the City was the arrival of Joe Duckworth (Blackburn Rovers), in the Cathedral City. The latter was really a grand half-back, one of the best in the country, but unfortunately enjoyed the reputation of being about the dirtiest, and not without cause either, but nevertheless he knew all the points of the game, and his tuition was invaluable to J. H. S. and his merry men.

Naturally the supporters of the team were more than annoyed. Inuendoes were knocking about, and for the first time on record, not a few offered their season tickets for sale. This was looked upon as a capital joke by the Committee, and arrangements were made to purchase them at a certain figure, but the bulk of the malcontents thought better of it, and wisely decided to assist the Committee to put the good old ship, Grimsby Town, on a firm basis.

For some time the Committee had been anything but a happy family, in a great measure attributable to a few of the players being on it, in fact some of them had the idea they were entitled to a certain amount of pay for their services, and yet passed as amateurs, so at length we had veiled professionalism in our midst. The result was that the coffers being empty at the termination of the season, it was decided to play a match for their benefit, which was duly arranged. No great difficulty was experienced in carrying it through. There was no close season, and the consequence was they received a certain amount of the all necessary.

This season instead of the six-a-side contests on Good Friday, the Town Committee decided to have a contest between the four best junior teams in the district, and the following teams were selected :— Cleethorpes Town, Perseverance, West Marsh Association and Humber Rovers, the prizes offered being 11 silver medals. After a grand contest the Humber Rovers won the medals, much to the delight of Charlie Parker, who practically ran the latter team.

With the termination of the season 1886-7 the Committee having been re-arranged a great deal of spade work was the order of the day. Meetings were held almost daily at Dring's Hotel, and to the surprise of the general public, a team was placed on the field on Whit Monday and Tuesday that was infinitely superior to any that had ever represented a club in the Fen County before. Here it is :—

Goal, G. Atkinson.

Backs, J. H. Taylor and H. Taylor.

Half-backs, W. Hopewell, J. Seal and R. Vamplew.

Right wing, H. Atkinson and W. May.

Centre, F. Geary.

Left wing, R. McBeth and L. Cooper.

Norman's Notts. team and the Wolverhampton Wanderers were their opponents, and both were defeated.

With some it remained a mystery how the service of such a team were secured, and so it remained, as the Committee, especially the Finance section, were very reticent, and quite right too, as in these days of veiled professionalism it was just like sitting on a volcano. It is satisfactory to note just now the Committee had regained the confidence of the general public, and the offer was given them by some of the leading supporters, that providing a powerful team could be organised they were prepared to put their hands down to any reasonable amount, and so they did. Yes, events in general were happening in a mysterious way, and one fine day a couple of strangers were espied in Cleethorpe Road. To our surprise (I don't think) they happened to be Jimmy Lundie and Johnny Lee. They declared they could play at football, and speedily gave us an illustration. What luck they should wander this way, wasn't it?

Let us look carefully at the new arrivals. McBeth, Cooper, Geary, Lee, Lundie, Riddoch, Vamplew and May. The latter were two good men, but still not the class of the others. What a six. If Tom Browell, the Hull centre, was worth £1,600, what was the value of these? I should imagine at least ten thousand pounds, and yet we secured them for about as many sovereigns. To those of the present generation a little of their records may be interesting. Here it is :—

BOB McBETH originally played for the Edinburgh St. Bernards and was one of the first to cross the border, with Hugh McIntyre, and Fergy Suter. Both the latter went to Blackburn Rovers and Bob to Accrington, then one of the leading clubs in the country, and he assisted them when they broke the record of Preston North End, then in the Zenith of their power, by defeating them after they had scored twenty consecutive wins. Of course, he came as an amateur. In fact, he got the licence of the Golden Fleece, where he stayed some years, but he told me that it was the nearest thing in the world that on arriving here he did not jump in the first train and return to Accrington. As luck would have it, he landed at the Town Station on Statute Day, and was so surprised at the appearance of the Country Johnnies that he had half a mind to turn back, but shortly after he was the first to acknowledge that the inhabitants of this quarter of the globe were anything but the innocents abroad he imagined.

COOPER, who came from Derby County, was on the small side. Thanks to the form shown by him in the six-a-side contests and ordinary matches we had our eye on him for some time, with the result that he donned the club colours. Speedy and clever on the ball, he, with McBeth were one of, if not the best left wings in the country. In fact, after an experience of thirty years, I can conscientiously say I have never seen a better.

FREDDY GEARY was more or less an unknown quantity, but the form shown by him when the Notts. Rangers paid their numerous visits was quite good enough, and when he settled down he proved a veritable terror. Possibly he was the fastest centre in the country, quite capable of doing evens, and when he migrated to Liverpool, where I believe he is to this day, he speedily became an International, and did not disgrace himself in that position.

JOHNNY LEE was a veritable surprise packet. In appearance he was about the most unlikely person you could imagine to be a footballer. He learnt his football with the Edinburgh Hibernians, and last season had helped them to win the Scottish Cup. Although an Edinburgh team they were the predecessors of the celebrated Celtic Club, so you can imagine the enthusiasm this win caused amongst the Irish paternity ayont the border. Fast and tricky as a monkey; truth to tell he was a very likely exponent of the Darwinian theory. His reception was great when he first visited our dear friends the City, and cries were immediately raised exhorting him to bring his tail with him. Johnny, however, took it in good part, and speedily proved that he could, at all events, play football.

JIMMY LUNDIE, who likewise assisted the Hibs. to win the Scottish Cup, was also an International on his merits. Without beating about the bush, it is exceedingly doubtful when he was at his best whether there was another back in the country to equal him. Cool, gentlemanly on the field to a degree, he scorned to take an advantage of a foe, and never during his career in the Fisheries was he known to give a foul. Why he retired so early passes my comprehension, as, even if he lost his pace to a great extent, his judgment was quite sufficient to merit his position in any team the calibre of Grimsby Town.

In a conversation with Jimmy on the herring slip he told me rather a good yarn. Before he came to the Fisheries he played for the Hibs. against the Corinthians, who were very strong just then. During the match one of the brothers Walters, the backs of the Corinthians, was injured, and as they were due to play Queen's Park the following day, which was looked upon then as practically equal to an International, they were in a very awkward position. As it happened Jimmy fairly bottled the opposing wing of the Corinthians, and to his surprise he was invited to make the journey to Glasgow and become a full blown Corinthian. Nothing loth, he consented, and did more than a little towards beating the Queen's Park. Naturally, the sons of Corinth were delighted and when the match was over, so was Jimmy. The operation was quite simple. He was called into the room where the sixteen Corinthians were and each of them dropped a sovereign into his hand, and J. L. landed 16 of the best. Very annoying wasn't it? In fact, it was better than veiled professionalism.

RIDDOCK, like McBeth, originally played for the Edinburgh St. Bernards. He was not only one of the best dribblers of the day, but very tricky, a magnificent shot for goal, plucky to a degree, and took any amount of stopping. In fact, for several seasons he was one of the best forwards in the country, and smiles when he sees the efforts of the players of the present day.

With prospects of the brightest we had yet another arrival in the Fisheries, a bird known as the Round Robin. It cannot be said that he was a welcome visitor, as, when he once, landed, he came to stay, and what was more annoying, caused any amount of friction amongst the various owners of the mysterious bird. Briefly speaking, it was the only way of raising the all necessary, and candidly it consisted of such a nice piece of paper, not very large, but it was simply marvellous the figures you could get on it. I well remember the meeting when the bird was introduced. A gentleman whose initials were A. B. was in the chair. It was gently handed up to him. After a careful perusal he said "If I sign this I shall be responsible for a sum of money." In vain we pleaded, he refused. Alas, he showed better judgement than some of us, and evidently he knew something. Shortly afterwards a knock came at the door, and a certain player appeared, who was duly introduced as a gentleman amateur. In vain those nearest to him endeavoured to give the tip. He failed to take it, and to our surprise said "That's all right, but what about the sanguinary money." Tableau, the chairman's face was a study. He departed hence, and we knew him no more.

Left to Right.—H. Atkinson, J. H. Taylor, H. Smith, R. Chapman, H. Taylor, W. T. Lammin, H. Monument, J. Lee, R. McBeth, J. Lundie, W. Hopewell, L. Cooper

D. Riddock, H. Smith, junr.

GRIMSBY TOWN F.C. TEAM, 1887.

All round a better class of ordinary matches was arranged, the principal teams being, Wolverhampton Wanderers, Derby County, Bolton Wanderers, Lockwood Bros., Notts County, Notts. Forest, Rossendale, Small Heath, Long Eaton Rangers, Mitchell St. George's, Stoke, &c. Fully represented they naturally extended our team, but the advantage of ground generally turned the scale. Any amount of excitement prevailed, and I was the victim on one occasion. It occurred in the Bolton Wanderers match. I was Referee. One of the latter team was supposed to fist a ball out, but I declined to give a free kick simply because if it did occur I did not see it, but all the same I had quite a lively time as possibly if the foul had been given our team might have scored and won the match.

One remarkable feature this season was that practically a team of goalkeepers appeared for Grimsby Town, inasmuch as no less than eight donned the colours. Here they are :— G. Atkinson, Kilvan, H. Smith, junior, Teddy McCormack, F. Christian, Houltby (Brog), C. H. Howlett and Hugh McIntyre. The latter was invited by McBeth to come down at Christmas time and keep goal against Owlerton. After the match the usual crowd assembled, and a lively time we had. As midnight approached we took the Christmas Carol business on. Sometimes it was appreciated, occasionally not, as for instance, when we landed at the only Ernest Michael Willy N—, the well-known timber merchant. He had retired, but, after the usual Christians Awake had been rendered, opening the bedroom window he invited us to wait until he descended. After a short interval he opened the door, but to our surprise greeted us with a shower of fire-irons. Mac said goalkeeping was a fool to it, and it was a sight for the gods to see us endeavouring to make our exit through a door about a yard wide. After this the crowd condescended to honour my house with their presence. I have a vivid recollection of about 28 being in our kitchen at the old show, 230 Victoria Street. Poor old Harry T. detected a false note in the harmony, rather surprising was it not, at this period of the evening. Eventually I persuaded them to retire, and having barred the doors, retired to enjoy a well earned night's repose.

Another arrival at the Fisheries was R. S. King, nephew of the late Bishop of Lincoln, who had been Captain of the Oxford University Team the previous year, occupying the position of right half-back. Naturally, his credentials were quite good enough, and I was deputed to wait upon him at his lodgings, the Church House, Queen Street, and asked him to give the town his services. He consented, but although competent enough, through various reasons he discontinued playing long ere the termination of the season.

At this period the rules affecting players were very vague, and being assisted by the prevalence of veiled professionalism, any player desiring to migrate had little difficulty in performing the operation. In comparison to other clubs we were distinctly lucky this season, as only Geary and Howlett of any note departed hence. The former went to Everton, and, eventually became an International, whilst the latter returned to Gainsborough, and after a time migrated to Sheffield United. In fact he was the first goalkeeper the latter club ever had.

During this season the first County match ever played in Grimsby took place at Abbey Park, Lincolnshire beating Yorkshire by four goals to one. It is satisfactory to note that no less than six locals played, H. Taylor, J. H. Taylor, W. Hopewell, H. Atkinson, and H. Monument, Grimsby Town, and Plumtree, Cleethorpes. A lot of dissatisfaction was expressed because Riddock, Lundie, McBeth, Cooper, &c., were not selected, but the explanation was simple enough. They were not eligible, as it was necessary to possess a two years' residential qualification ere you were eligible to represent the County.

Naturally the greatest interest was centred in the cup competitions, and once more we found ourselves in the Fourth Round of the National. Having easily beaten our opponents in the first round we had the luck to have a by in the second but in the third were drawn against our dear friends the City at home. Of course the excitement was great, and it was felt that records would easily be beaten in the matter of attendance and likewise the all necessary. Preparations were made to accommodate them, extra stands were erected, and when the eventful day arrived at least 6,000 people were gathered round the enclosure, the takings being about £180. Neither McBeth nor Cooper played, not being eligible, Morton, from Louth, and Charlie Soames, Humber Rovers, filling the vacancies. To the delight of the majority of the spectators, after a tremendous struggle the Town got the upper hand of the City, the latter being beaten by two to none.

In the fourth round we were drawn to meet the Old Foresters at

Kennington Oval, but once more our friend J. H. S. handed in a protest to the English Association in Veiled Professionalism and Importation. As a natural consequence the Association appointed a commission to sit at Sheffield, consisting of Smith (Derby), Jessop (Notts)., and David Haigh (Sheffield), always a good friend to Grimsby Town. As usual J. H. S. spared no expense in his attempt to humble Grimsby Town, but once more he failed. It was positively amusing to hear Jimmy Lundie and Johnny Lee explain how they wandered South in search of work. Talk about the Innocents Abroad, they were not in it. Eventually the following verdict was returned :— "That Lincoln City had signally failed to prove their case of importation and Grimsby Town were awarded the tie." If necessary J. H. S. could have caught it warm, as Fred Geary was present, and was prepared to swear that he was offered a bribe to give evidence against Grimsby Town.

After this long interval, perhaps, it is immaterial if the impeachment of importation is acknowledged, and the Grimsby Town Committee had an anxious time before the eventful day arrived for the meeting to be held. All this was caused by the simplest thing in the world, viz., the presence of one sentence bang in the centre of the minute book, which would have convicted us forthwith, but the Committee rose to the occasion, and simply decided that it would be just as well if a fresh minute book was obtained, and the whole lot re-written with the exception of the fatal paragraph, and it took a lot of doing, let me tell you, during the short period before the meeting was held. However, by staying up at night, arranging for the various chairmen to attend and append their signatures everything promised well, the only drawback being the new appearance of the book, both the cover, leaves and ink. This was got over by dirtying the cover somewhat by sitting on it, etc., rubbing the leaves and holding the ink to the fire to make it look older. Although the Committee looked at it carefully and smiled, it came off all right. Not a bad wheeze, was it?

After all this trouble it was hoped we should beat the Foresters at the Oval, but it was not to be, as they beat us four to two. On the play there was nothing like this in it. As a matter of fact, the match was to a great extent lost by playing Christian in preference to George Atkinson in goal. The former naturally had not had the experience George had of playing in Cup Ties, and the back division likewise had not the confidence they would have had if

George had been between the sticks, and to this to a great extent I attributed the loss of the match.

Having finished with the National, our attention was centred in the Lincolnshire Cup, and naturally both the players and the Committee were anxious to secure the trophy once more. We got through the early rounds easy enough, and our friends of Gainsborough relieved the City of any further interest by beating them in the semi-final, but even then J. H. S. was not satisfied and made Horncastle the cats-paw this journey in his attempt to wreck Grimsby Town. Meeting Horncastle away (by-the-bye, this was the first time Ambrose Langley played against the Town), they were defeated two to one, but just by way of a change a protest was lodged on the grounds that several of the players were not eligible. A meeting was duly held and the protest was sustained, and Grimsby Town fined £5 for expenses incurred. Strange to say they were not disqualified. Oh, dear no, their presence was required in the final as wherever they played a great following was assured, and therefore to the surprise and disgust of all concerned we were allowed to meet Gainsborough Trinity Recreationists, and beat them. In the meantime J.H.S. had unearthed a letter which had been sent to one of our team promising him a job on the Great Central Railway which he has to this day if he played for Grimsby Town. This was, of course, veiled professionalism pure and simple. The clouds were gathering quickly, and at our committee meeting it was decided to obtain the original letter if possible. How this was obtained is immaterial, suffice to say we got it, and I had it in my pocket when I represented the Town Club at the meeting. When this took place I had a copy of the letter shown me. Being a bit deaf I had not heard the Chairman announce it was only a copy, but I at once said I was prepared to swear that it was not our Secretary's writing. Of course, I did not insinuate anything wrong, but clearly if the original could not be found the case must collapse, and so it did. After the meeting was over there were ructions below in the smoke-room of the Queen's, and this was another occasion when it was necessary to have a bodyguard to escort us to the station. How we did love each other in these days.

As a consequence the City resigned from the Association, and eventually they were so disgusted at the conduct of certain of the Committee of the Association that Gainsborough did likewise, and the consequence was that

after all there was no final, and the Cup was held in abeyance. To decide
which was the better team of the two home and home matches were arranged
between the two finalists, Grimsby Town and Gainsborough Trinity. The first
ended in favour of the town by six to one, and Gainsborough won the return
by one to nil. The City were determined to have their revenge, and decided
not to play the return fixture with the Town until we sent them ten pounds
more share of gate of the English Cup. Clearly they were in the wrong this
journey, but after all it is only fair to state that a year or two previous we
owed them a match, and therefore they only returned a Roland for an Oliver.
After the above protest I think you will agree with, me that to a great extent
the Cup-ties were won in the Committee Room. Yes, the office was no sinecure,
and without blowing the trumpet unduly, I should imagine that if Manchester
United and Middlesbrough last season had had a Directorate of a similar
calibre they would not have experienced such a rough time at the hands of
the Association.

Amongst the items which caused not a little anxiety was the illness of the
bird alluded to in one of the previous columns. Although he had grown
enormously he had become very restive, and it was only by careful attention
that he did not collapse. Additional advice, however, having been obtained
he recovered somewhat, much to the relief of all concerned. Unfortunately
it was only temporary, and eventually he flew away. How this was
accomplished I will endeavour to relate as briefly as possible. At Easter time
we had some excellent gates, and having realised a substantial sum of money,
a few of us entered a certain building and discharged the liability of the
club. At the Committee meeting there was an awful row with a certain section,
but even they eventually agreed it was the simplest operation in the world to
spend money when you are not responsible for the all necessary, and we all
of us present, some sixteen, agreed to sign a fresh guarantee to the bank,
with the result that a second round Robin appeared, a very fine bird, and
much larger than the previous one.

With the lease of the Clee Park grounds rapidly drawing to a close, I
brought forward a scheme for nothing less than the purchase, making it
freehold, of the whole of the Clee Park Gardens. To those who had not even
seen the light of day at this period, it may be interesting to give them some
idea of the size of the grounds. They extended from Park Street to Phelps

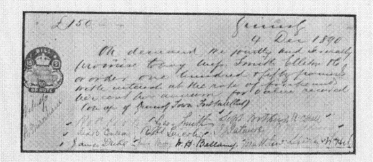

THE BIRD.

Street on the one hand, and from Cleethorpe Road to Harrington Street, taking in both Montague and Taylor streets, thus the ground was practically square. Even to this day a portion of the old cinder track can be seen on the eight foot at the road of the Phelps Street houses, also one or two of the trees that were in the gardens on the boundary.

It may be interesting to note that Park Street, Hamilton Street, in fact, the great majority of the streets to the right nearly up to Bath Street, were green fields, likewise, of course the whole of New Cleethorpes, so the rising generation will have some idea how this district has developed within the last quarter of a century.

My idea was to have a really first-class Athletic Club embracing grounds for cricket, football, brasses and quoits, cinder tracks for cycling and running, and a gymnasium. With this object in view I drew a plan showing the Clee Park Hotel, exactly where it is, and the various grounds encircled by a half-mile cinder track. The gymnasium was to be built at the Harrington Street end, the frontage to form a grand stand. With this plan I interviewed the late W. T. Hewitt, who thought it a capital idea, and asked me if I would become a full-blown landlord if he built a first-class hotel at the corner, an honour which I declined.

Just then there was any amount of enthusiasm in the town over the scheme. I had obtained about 300 promises of membership, the majority of whom were in a position to put their hands down if necessary. Meetings were called at the Temperance Hall where I unfolded my scheme. These were attended by the leading athletes of the town in all branches, and to all appearance the scheme was a "dead cert," but alas, you never know your luck, and just when it was on the threshold of success it became a total wreck, in a great measure attributable to the jealousy then existing between the two Cyclists' Clubs, the present Cyclist Club and the Yarborough. Clearly this was a tremendous error, and it is certainly interesting to imagine what the value of the ground would have been at the present day.

In the season 1887 and 1888 the chief item in the football world was the formation of the Football League, which was the inception of Mr. McGregor, of Birmingham. From the very first it was a tremendous success, and naturally had a detrimental effect on the prospects of clubs the calibre of Grimsby Town, which in previous years had been able to secure visits without any great difficulty from the leading clubs of the day. For the sake of reference I append the list of clubs that formed it. Here they are :— Everton, Wolverhampton Wanderers, West Bromwich Albion, Aston Villa, Blackburn Rovers, Accrington, Burnley, Stoke, Notts. County and Derby County.

At the end of this season the executive were not particularly anxious to call a general meeting to discuss the balance sheet, in fact they quite forgot — (Oh, that new bird) — and instead, the members were informed that a copy of the balance sheet could be obtained from the Secretary by payment of 6d. Not a bad idea, was it? I don't suppose many ventured to pay the 6d., and if they did, I venture to predict that not one in the dozen understood it, neither did we particularly want them to either.

One noticeable item was the large quantity of "salmon" consigned to the fisheries, the first arrivals including Ogilvie, Mudie, Hunt, Hislop and Sutherland. Later on Lundie requiring a little fresh air, journeyed North with his angling apparatus. Thanks to a friend of the Club I don't think the Scottish Press were notified of his arrival, and he was shadowed. Nevertheless he landed a beauty, no less than Dan Doyle. Evidently the bait was very strong, and attractive, just now. Considering that Wally Reid, by some means or other, was also landed shortly after, the net seemed fairly full, and what a haul it was.

Without discounting the merits of the others, Doyle, Ogilvie, Sutherland and Reid were clearly the pick. Dan Doyle, with Jimmy Lundie, were in my opinion almost the best backs in England, although the brothers Walters for the Corinthians were still in their prime. Unfortunately Dan never settled in the Fisheries, migrating, after the accident to Cropper, to Bolton Wanderers. Afterwards he crossed the border once more, played International, got into the Glasgow City Council, and became of some importance in the civic world. Just after the Ibrox disaster, happening to be in Glasgow, I tried to have an interview with him, went to his club, but unfortunately just missed him.

Adam Ogilvie, without a doubt, was about the straightest Scotchman that ever crossed the border, scorned to take advantage of any club, a magnificent all round player, half-back, full-back, or in goal. Eventually he migrated to Blackburn Rovers and kept a brilliant goal for them several seasons.

Donald Sutherland was of quite a similar stamp, and was a faithful servant to the Club. Distinctly above the average in ability as a forward or half-back he did any amount of work of a very clean character. Eventually he left Grimsby, but returned to work at his trade as a joiner. Judge of my surprise when, after an interval of some fourteen years, he landed on a job of mine to fix some houses out. Evidently he likes the fishing port, as he is still here working at his trade.

Reid was of a somewhat different stamp, although there was no doubting his ability, indeed he was a grand player in any part of the back division. Unfortunately, he became rather too fond of that common disease, lifting the elbow, and the consequence was that he disappeared from the football world when comparatively a young man.

Considering the League had been formed, a really capital list of ordinary fixtures had been arranged, the principal clubs being Bolton Wanderers, Sunderland, Long Eaton Rangers, Derby Midland, Halliwell, Burnley, Northwich Victoria, &c. Possibly the warmest of the lot was that against Bolton Wanderers, and to say the least they were surprised when they were so easily defeated. Naturally they wanted their revenge, and later on invited us into Lancashire. Nothing loth we consented. An excursion was run, and it was well patronised, this being Grimsby Town's first visit to the County Palatine. After a tremendous struggle they defeated us five to three, but our team made a great impression in Lancashire, which we fondly hoped would be of some service afterwards to the Club. Then as now, we arranged to have tea in Manchester, and singular to relate, met Johnny Lee, wearing the green, it being St. Patrick's eve. This necessitated wetting the saint, an operation to which I have no recollection of hearing anyone object. Hugh McIntyre, who had piloted us in Manchester decided to make the journey home with us, and he did not forget it for many a day. No, everything was all solid, especially the toys. What with the customary games of nap, solo whist, &c., songs, and impromptu dances the lights of Grimsby Town were seen all too quickly, and we dispersed delighted with our first visit to Lancashire.

In the midst of all our triumphs it is satisfactory to note that the services of Harry Taylor to Grimsby Town were not forgotten, and Sam Norman brought a team from Nottingham to play a match at the Park for his benefit. This was not treated seriously from a playing point of view, but the public rallied round Harry sufficiently to prove that his services to Grimsby Town were appreciated in the Fisheries.

After our wholesale landing of "salmon" it could scarcely be expected that inducements would not be offered to our players, but bar Doyle going to Bolton, nothing particular happened except concerning Billy H—. He, indeed, was a bird of passage. Here's the programme :— Went to the City, left them for Derby County, returned to us, then City once more. Not bad was it, but then he was an amateur, don't you know?

During the Christmas and New Year holidays it was determined by the Committee to hold a carnival and matches were arranged with the following teams :— Motherwell and Clyde, both Glasgow, the first Scottish visit to the Fisheries, Derby Midland, Northwich Victoria, Burnley and Halliwell. Considering they won four of these, and drew the other two, I think you will agree with me that the lemon kali must have been conspicuous by its absence at this festive period of the year.

Bob McBeth was so delighted at the form shown by the team that on January 2nd he invited the whole of them, Committee, &c., of Grimsby Town to be his guests at the Golden Fleece Hotel. Needless to say we enjoyed ourselves. Everything was of the best, and it was a treat for the gods to hear us give Auld Lang Syne. With a strong Scotch contingent, amongst whom was our old friend Hugh McIntyre present, it went with a swing, assisted by a wee drappie of Scotch, don't you know.

Unfortunately this, certainly the best season up to date, was marred by the sad accident to Cropper, when playing for Staveley at Clee Park. During the match Doyle and he collided, and accidentally Dan caught him in the stomach with his knee. At the time it was not thought serious. He was conveyed across the road to Charlie Parker's Cocoa House, at the corner of Park Street, but although he had the best of medical attention, and poor old R. C. Hall and others sat up with him all night, he died. Truly it was a sad termination of a very promising career, especially in the cricket field, as he played for Derbyshire and had already scored a couple of centuries against Yorkshire in one match. Determined to see it through, Grimsby Town were represented at the grave side by I. J. Patmore, the secretary, and Bob McBeth, and a suitable stone was erected, the Victoria Cricket Club Committee voting their balance left over when the club was disbanded to pay for it. Dan Doyle, although it was a pure accident, never cared to play at the Park again, and as mentioned above, gave the Bolton Wanderers the benefit of his services.

It is not my intention to dwell upon the Lincolnshire Cup. Truth to tell, little interest was taken in it simply through Lincoln City and Gainsborough Trinity resigning from the competition, but when Grimsby Town appeared at Lincoln to play the Rangers, the conduct of the crowd was scandalous. In fact after the match was over the team had the greatest difficulty in getting away without injury. The Lincoln City Committee afterwards apologised, but it was very evident to the veriest novice that a considerable amount of ill-feeling still existed amongst the followers of Lincoln City against Grimsby Town.

After this fiasco it is a pleasure to note that we had a brilliant career in our efforts to annex the National Trophy. Singular to relate, once more we were drawn against the City in the first round at Clee Park. Result: A draw. We duly met at Lincoln. Once more a draw. Our dear friend, J. H. S., handed the usual protest in on the question of Doyle not being eligible and claimed that the match should be re-played at Lincoln. However, once more he was wrong in the opinion of the Association, and it was ordered to be re-played at Bramall Lane, Sheffield, with neutral umpires and referee. J. C. Clegg, the present President of the Football Association, was the referee. Result : Town beat the City once more by three goals to one. It is satisfactory to note that after this protest the Committee of Grimsby Town thought it quite as well to ask the English Association why Lincoln City had not paid the expenses of last year's protest. Result : They were ordered to pay forthwith. Yes, J. H. S. was enjoying himself just now.

Soon afterwards there were ructions amongst the City. An Independent Committee was formed, with J. W., who afterwards became manager for Newton Heath, as Chairman, and it was proved up to the hilt that Lincoln City was simply a private club run by a syndicate. Of course, this being so, all the team were ineligible to compete for the English Cup. A fine opportunity for Grimsby Town, but the Committee scorned to take advantage of it, and, truth to tell, would rather have given them a lift in the football world.

The second round saw Newark easily beaten, after a draw The Meg Islanders suffered a similar operation in the third, but in the fourth we ran up against a very powerful team, Sunderland Albion. Fortunately, it was at Clee Park, and after a tremendous struggle they were defeated. Our form was so good that no less an authority than R. P. Gregson, when we saw him and his colleagues off at the station, expressed the opinion that he fully expected to see 'us in the semi-final. I append the teams and officials :—

GRIMSBY TOWN.
Goal, Houltby.
Backs, Lundie and D. Doyle.
Half-backs, J. H. Taylor, H. Smith, Wally Reid.
Forwards, J. Taylor, jun., D. Sutherland, D. Riddock, R. McBeth and J. Hunt.

SUNDERLAND ALBION.
Goal, Angus.
Backs, Moore and MacFarlane.
Half-Backs, Richardson, Murray and Hastings.
Forwards, Kilpatrick, Stewart, McLellan, J. Stewart and McMunn.
Umpires, T. Duxbury, Darwen, and D. Woolfall, Blackburn Rovers.
Referee, R. P. Gregson, Blackburn Rovers.

A careful perusal of the above list proves, that we were not the only team importing Scotch "salmon."

In the fifth round the pace became hotter still, as we were drawn to meet no less a team than Preston North End, then in the zenith of their power. Of course great preparations were made, new stands erected, and everything pointed to a record gate. Unfortunately the elements interfered. It was terribly cold, and the consequences was that the attendance was affected. From the first the pace was a cracker, and when Grimsby shot the first goal, Sutherland doing the needful, the excitement was tremendous. Unfortunately it was disallowed, a mistake in my opinion. This had a demoralising effect on our team, and North End scoring twice, won the tie. On the play there was precious little in it, and if Grimsby Town had been allowed the first goal there is little doubt they would have relieved the North End of any anxiety re the destination of the Cup for this season.

The following were the teams :—

FEBRUARY 16TH, 1889.
PRESTON NORTH END.
Goal, Mills Roberts.
Backs, Howarth and Holmes.
Half-backs, Drummond, Russell and Graham.
Forwards, right-wing, Thompson and Dewhurst.

Centre, Goodall. ,
Left-wing, Ross and Gordon.

GRIMSBY TOWN.
Goal, Houltby.
Backs, Lundie and Doyle.
Half-backs, J. H. Taylor, H. Smith and W. Reid.
Forwards, right-wing, J. Taylor, jun., and G. Sutherland.
Centre, D. Riddock.
Left-wing, M. McBeth and J. Hunt.
Umpires, Stacey and Wilkinson.
Referee, J. C. Clegg (Sheffield).

The semi-final, North End versus the Throstles being fixed for Sheffield, an excursion was arranged, and a lot of us journeyed to the cutlery capital to see the match, the bulk of us investing 2s. 6d. to obtain a good seat, which, of course, was numbered. Unfortunately the train was late, and when we arrived I should imagine there would be quite 30,000 present. Luckily for myself I happened to be with a future chief constable of the Fishery Town. His card had a wonderful effect upon the policeman in charge, and the result was that we got perched on the top of the grand stand. I shall not forget the sight in a hurry. It was the first time I had ever seen mounted police on the field, but they were very useful, as the crowd utterly refused to keep their position, and repeatedly encroached on the field.

Through business reasons Mr. Lammin resigned his position as secretary, after holding it from the inception of the club. What the followers of the club owe him for guiding the good ship Grimsby Town through the stormy waters it encountered during its career will never be known, but they can take it from me that he was a secretary distinctly above the average, knowing his alphabet from A to Z. Fortunately he was succeeded by another good man, I. J. P., who had already enjoyed a lengthy experience on the Committee, and therefore was fully up in the intricate points so frequently cropping up concerning the interests of the club.

In the close season application was made for a position in the League, but sad to relate they did not receive a single vote. At the meeting of the formation of the Alliance, they were more successful. The Midland teams tried hard to keep both us and Sunderland Albion out, but Lancashire were

Photo by]

Left to Right—J. H. Taylor, W. Reid, J. Lundie, Houlthy, H. Smith, A. Ogilvie,
D. Sutherland, J. Taylor, junr., D. Riddock, K. McBeth, J. Hunt.

GRIMSBY TOWN CUP TEAM AGAINST PRESTON NORTH END, 1889.

[Louthian Bros., Grimsby.

our friends, and we were elected. Not, however, without that absurd stipulation that owing to our situation (geographical) we were to pay half the railway fares of our opponents, and Sunderland Albion three-quarters. However, so far as we were concerned, we had achieved our object. A capital list of fixtures was assured for next season, and we returned home with a double-six smile — one that didn't wear off in a day or two either. The following were the teams selected for the League and Alliance :—

LEAGUE.

Everton, Wolves, Preston North End, Throstles, Bolton Wanderers, Derby County, Accrington, Burnley, Aston Villa, Stoke, Notts. County, Blackburn Rovers.

ALLIANCE.

Bootle, Crewe Alexandra, Walsall Town, Sunderland Albion, Sheffield Wednesday, Notts. Forest, Newton Heath, Small Heath, Darwen, Long Eaton Rangers, Grimsby Town, Lincoln City.

In connection with the grand work done by the team during the first season it is some consolation to note that all the credit does not belong to the "salmon" imported from bonnie Scotland; oh dear, no, as Houltby, the two Smiths, Jack and Harry, and Jack Taylor, junior, quite upheld the reputation of local football. The two Smiths, as half backs put in a tremendous amount of work. Taylor, junior, a local product from the Humber Rovers, now a shoemaker in Oxford Street, improved wonderfully, and was quite worth his place in the team, whilst Houltby who rejoiced in the appelation of McBrog of the Isle, was practically impregnable in goal, not a few of his opponents giving him a wide berth, and not without reason too. He had one qualification only possessed by one other goalkeeper I ever saw, Willie Foulks, the 24 stone custodian of Sheffield United, viz., he could pick up the football with one hand and throw it a tremendous distance, a performance which generally staggered the opposing forwards. After the selection of the Alliance Clubs they petitioned the Railway Companies for a reduction of fares for teams, asking for a single fare for the double journey. After consideration they decided not to accede to the request — a serious matter for Grimsby Town, as it meant a difference of some forty to fifty pounds in railway fares alone.

However, thanks to our form of the previous season, we had the good fortune to be exempted from the Qualifying Rounds of the English Competition. This I attribute to a great extent to a good word or two put in for us by the Lancashire contingent on the Board of the Association, Messrs. Gregson, Duxbury, etc., who had more than once officiated in the Cup Ties we were engaged in. There is an old adage that all work and no play makes Jack a dull boy, and therefore the Town Committee thought it highly necessary that Reid and Sutherland should have a holiday across the border. Apparently they had a good time, angling for "salmon" being their particular sport. It cannot be denied they had some fairly good sport, and the result was another consignment of, "salmon." It consisted at various periods of Davie Black, Johnny McKnight, Ross, Turnbull, McDill and Findley. Of these the four latter were nothing out of the ordinary, and when they departed hence their places were easily filled, but the remaining pair were well worth keeping.

Davie Black was a Scotch International, tricky to a degree, a magnificent outside left, but suffered from being rather on the small side, whilst Johnny McKnight, who had the making of a very good centre-forward, absolutely declined to train, and the consequence was that he was very seldom in condition, which caused him to disappear from the football field muck earlier than he need have done.

With the termination of the lease of Clee Park, and the difficulty of securing a suitable pitch, the Town Committee were placed in a serious position, but a certain lawyer came to the rescue and induced Mr. Heneage to grant us a seven years' lease of a plot of land in Welholme Road, adjoining the Park, between it and the railway, the understanding being that on no consideration could the lease be renewed, as already the surrounding land had been spoken for building purposes.

Ever progressive, the Committee, assisted by some of the leading lights of the town, agreed to have a ground that would compare favourably with those of the leading clubs of the day. Mr. W. Waller was engaged to take the levels and super-intend the drainage. The laying of the ground, stands, etc., was secured by Mr. C. Simons. Timber, wire ropes, etc., to go round the ground were either given by friends or provided at a nominal cost, and the result was that when the season commenced Grimsby Town possessed one of the best appointed football grounds in the kingdom. After these improvements and the admission into the Alliance, naturally it was necessary to have a revised list of charges, and the following scale was adopted :—

	£	s.	d.
Season tickets admit to reserved portion..........		10	0
Season tickets admit all matches to reserved portion		15	0
Season tickets admit all matches to reserved portion of grand stand	1	1	0
Season tickets Ladies' reserved side		7	6
Season tickets Ladies' reserved side including stand		10	6

West Bromwich, one of the leading Clubs of the day, had the honour of opening the ground, and to everybody's surprise, were defeated by no less than six goals to one. This caused a great sensation throughout the country, and everybody interested in the game predicted a good season for the Town, but unfortunately by some means or other the promise was scarcely fulfilled, although at the same time it cannot be denied they fully held their own in the various competitions they engaged in.

One result of our brilliant Cup Tie career and admission to the Alliance was that ordinary matches were a thing of the past as far as attracting the public, except perhaps at holiday times. To fill up the vacant dates, however, it was necessary to have some, and the result that home and away matches were arranged with the City, which, however, caused nothing like the excitement of previous years. Whilst on the subject of the Cits, it may be as well to note that this season they won the Championship of the Midland League. Another noticeable item was that the Town retired from the County Cup Competition. I don't suppose for one moment on any consideration would they have competed, but one absurd rule of the Association put the extinguisher on the idea, as it simply prevented Turnbull, Reid, Ogilvie, Sutherland, Ross, McKnight and Black from being eligible.

This season Davie Riddock took another match on, viz., he decided to get married. The Directorate were naturally interested in the matter, and by a subscription presented him with a capital Gladstone bag, and a substantial sum of money.

Then, as now, one of the most attractive matches in the Alliance was the annual visit to the Goose Fair to play Notts. Forest. This journey it was distinctly above the average, and there was indeed a veritable gathering of the clans, as no less than four teams, Notts. Forest, Notts. County, Stoke and Grimsby Town met at the Maypole. Well, to say the least, we had a good time. To hear the language an average visitor might have thought he was in Scotland, but as a matter of fact the one item that reminded me of across the border was the fluid, and I will admit there was more than a little knocking about that night.

At Christmas time one Alliance and two ordinary fixtures were arranged, Small Heath (Alliance), Notts. Forest, and London Casuals. All of them were won, the most noticeable item being the appearance of C. B. Fry in the Casuals as full-back. He also consented to assist us occasionally, thanks to Harry Mundahl, but, unfortunately, he was never able to accept the invitation when it was given. Little did we think when we saw him that he would develop into the greatest athlete that ever lived, but he did. International at football and cricket, even now, when I am writing this, 13 years after, his services would be invaluable in Australia. He also occupied the same position in the athletic world, could do practically evens for 100 yards, jump 6ft. 4ins. high, and 23ft. 4ins. long, besides excelling in racquets, lawn tennis, etc. Very warm, wasn't he?

As a contrast to the Notts. Forest match on Goose Fair day perhaps a word or two re the Alliance with Newton Heath at Ardwick will be interesting. Although I have knocked about the country thirty years, either as a volunteer, or a player, umpire, linesman, referee, or follower of cricket, football and other sports, I can honestly say I never saw such a ground, or experienced such a day as this. The ground, utterly devoid of grass, was literally under water. It rained in torrents throughout the game, and the players and myself, as umpire, were indeed a sight for the gods when the referee blew his whistle. We had no time to dress; jumped straight into a large drag; were driven straight to London Road Station and staggered not a few of the passengers when we rushed across the station to board our saloon. We were literally a mass of mud from head to foot. Buckets of water had been placed in the saloon and for about twenty miles of the journey homewards we were busily engaged having a wash, and changing. Luckily R. C. Hall had lent me his mackintosh to umpire in, but the pants, &c., were in a terrible state, and they were deposited in a heap with players' knickers, and I journeyed home with a rug round the lower extremities. After this, few will deny that we had earned our tea and something afterwards. Well, as usual, a capital list of toys, &c., were on board. It was simply marvellous how the pork pies and doorsteps (sandwiches) disappeared, and afterwards something else. Of course we protested on the state of the ground.

We were now on the eve of the English Cup, and it is rather singular that it was left for Lincoln City and Gainsborough Trinity to decide the winner of the qualifying round in this division, and enter the competition proper. Lincoln City were successful, and once more there was just a chance that we should meet again in the competition, but it was not to be, as we were drawn against Newcastle West End at Newcastle.

On the night before the match I. J. P. and myself represented the Club at a meeting of the Alliance held at the Clarence Hotel, Sheffield, when our protest against Newton Heath ground was heard. Of course, I had to give evidence, and said I was under the impression that we were playing on a portion of the new Manchester Canal, and assured the Committee that the shareholders of the above could always rely on having sufficient water, if that day was any criterion, to float the biggest battleship we had. They smiled but granted our request to have the match played over again. We won it, and no doubt this caused us to finish in the first four at the end of the season. After all this was not the most important business. For some time there had been wholesale migration of players and both the League and the Alliance thought it was high time the effectual stopper should be put on it. With this object the present meeting was called, and the following resolution, which had already been passed by the League, was passed :— "Before any player can be transferred from one League club to another, he must have the written consent of the Club with which he is engaged." This, of course, only applied to the League and Alliance, and unfortunately did not affect powerful clubs like Sunderland, &c., but the latter clubs were given the straight tip of the consequences if they continued to poach on our preserves, and for a time the resolution had a good effect and helped to purify the game to a certain extent.

I. J. P. and myself, having arranged to join the team at York, and journey with them up North to play Newcastle West End, found we had only a quarter of an hour to catch the train, and hastily summoning a cab, offered the cabby a shilling if he caught the train. By desperate efforts he did, but he had wrung it on us properly, as we found out afterwards that the hotel was quite adjacent to the station and he had simply run us round a square or two.

It was indeed a merry party that left York, for had we not won the protest, and having landed at Durham just at midnight, we made our way to the Three Tuns Hotel, where a glass of cherry brandy was already poured out for us, twenty all told. To those who have not visited this locality it may be as well to remark that the Three Tuns is one of the most celebrated hotels in the North, and for ages it has been customary to have a glass of cherry brandy for every guest on arrival. Some might object, but this journey I can assure you, they disappeared rapidly, also the supper consisting chiefly — Yes, I could a tale unfold concerning them, but perhaps it is quite as well to keep it dark.

Having to make all arrangements re the match at Newcastle, I.J.P. and I were up early, and departed hence leaving the team, &c., in bed. On arriving at Newcastle we made for St. James' Park, and to our surprise found the ground arrangements of quite a primitive character, nothing like ours in appointments or general appearances. Having tested it, we left to find a suitable crib for tea after the match, and a fearful mess we made of it. Up to then I thought I was a bit of a judge where to pitch your tent and enjoy yourself amongst the toys, but just for once we were well had, and it was about the worst spread our team sat down to.

Re the match. It was one of the most peculiar I ever saw. It blew a gale of wind across the field, and the consequence was that nearly all the play was confined to one half of the ground. At half time the game hung in the balance, and the team and a few of us had a consultation. It was pointed out that if one of the Newcastle forwards kept on the field throughout the game we might easily lose, but by some means or other he did not, and we won by the odd goal, a good performance. In the second round luck was dead against us, and we were drawn to play away from home at Blackburn against the Rovers. After a desperate struggle in which Adam Ogilvie distinguished himself greatly between the sticks, we were defeated, but all the same we fully extended the future Cup holders.

Just now, having become somewhat tired of "salmon" we thought it was wise to try a little local talent. The result was a couple of local lads were unearthed, who were destined to have quite a distinguished career in the colours of Grimsby Town. I allude to Alf and Hickey Rose, but certainly the most notable capture was Ambrose Langley, from Horncastle. I well remember the day when he made his first appearance at Abbey Park. Before the match we instructed Jimmy Lundie to give Adam a chance to test his abilities. At half-time we asked Jimmy what he thought of it. He said "D——it, he is better than I am." Of course he was not, but nevertheless even when quite a youngster he was a very good man. How he developed is now a matter of history. With us, Middlesbrough Ironopolis, Sheffield Wednesday, and Hull City he had a brilliant career, and it can safely be said that no club ever had a more steady and reliable player on its books.

For the Easter Carnival no less than six teams were engaged, Birmingham St. George's, Crewe Alexander, Clapton, Gainsborough Trinity, Bootle and Newton Heath. Considering that no less than five Reserves were called upon it is satisfactory to note that five matches were won and one drawn, fourteen goals scored for and seven against. It will be noted that one of the teams was Crewe Alexandra, who enjoyed considerable notoriety just now being known as the heroes of the two-foot rule. I have so frequently been asked about the why and the wherefore of this title that perhaps it may be quite as well to relate how they obtained it. They were playing in an English Cup Tie against the London Swifts, and after it was lost thought it just as well to measure the height of the goal posts. To their surprise they were three inches short, and they protested. Hence the title.

For some time during the season the form shown by certain of the Scotchmen particular had been anything but satisfactory, and it was the predominant subject at several Committee meetings. Of course, the opinions varied, but it was generally conceded that a few of the players not only took advantage of a certain privilege they had re their employment but would not train, one in particular very often spending the day in bed under the plea of sickness. As a remedy it was suggested that I paid the wages on Saturday, and deducted what I thought was fair for loss of time, etc. The day duly arrived. After the match I went into the dressing-room and asked Cob what he wanted. He said "I am not a sanguinary oatmeal eater." Of course he received his at once, as never had a club a straighter man than he. J. L. Adam, and the bulk of the others were all right, but when D. B. and J. McK. appeared I utterly refused to pay them more than a certain amount. They refused it, and announced their intention of taking a ticket for Glasgow. I advised them when they arrived to continue their journey and go to —— well, not Cleethorpes, but a somewhat warmer climate, They only went as far as Glasgow though. There was an awful row at our meeting. Some said that I had ruined the club, but the bulk of the Committee sided with me and instructions were sent to them to return in time for the Saturday's match, or they would be suspended for the rest of the season. They came back and, what is more, had to pay their own fare. Afterwards they behaved themselves somewhat better, and the consequence was that we eventually finished fairly well up in the Alliance, notwithstanding a temporary loss of form in the middle of the season. The results will bear inspection considering the calibre of the clubs met. In the Alliance we finished fourth. Here they are :—

Matches				Goals		
Played	Won	Drawn	Lost	For	Against	Points
22	12	8	 2	 58	47	 26

In all matches.

47	28	 13	 6	120	87

Not bad was it?

At the meeting of the Alliance there were any amount of applications for the four vacant positions, including Lincoln City, but there was only one alteration, viz., Stoke took the place of Long Eaton Rangers, who were perhaps quite as strong as ever, but were not in a position to have consignments of "salmon" to strengthen the team.

Naturally there was any amount of interest taken in the general meeting, and it was duly held at the Masonic Hall on June 20th, Mr. J. W. in the chair surrounded by about sixty others. After the Secretary's report re the successful season, the balance sheet was passed as follows :—

	£	s.	d.
Disbursements	2,026	3	6
Receipts	1,786	4	8
Balance	£239	18	10
Assets : Value of stands, &c	161	14	6
Balance against	£78	14	6

It will be interesting to some of the present generation to know that the average gate money received at these Alliance matches was under fifty-six pounds, and in those days we had a team at least the calibre of the present one. When this is considered, surely the difficulties experienced by the old directorates will be recognised and some little credit be given them for succeeding in keeping their club afloat.

To those not in the know apparently a very sensible proposition was made and seconded. It was to the effect that it would be more business-like and more satisfactory to all concerned if in the future all cash was paid into the bank, and nothing paid away except by cheque. This looked all solid, but alas, it was not workable, simply because the majority of the team required their share of the gate immediately after the match in current coin of the realm, don't you know?

For some time an opinion had been afloat that the Directorate were having a good time, they were not doing it for nothing, and so on, and not a few of those present announced their intention of getting in to partake of the good things knocking about. It therefore fairly staggered them when the Chairman, before the selection of the Committee, made the following remarks. He said the next business was the election of a secretary, treasurer and Committee, but before the latter was selected he had an explanation to make, a simple one, and it was this :— That the Committee sign a round robin (Oh, that bird) to the bank for whatever they may want during the ensuing year. Anyone coming fresh on the Committee would knock someone out, and the person coming on would have to take his place. It was fair to make this explanation then there would be no mistake. After this there was no particular rush amongst the budding aspirants. Before the election of officers it was announced to the regret of all present that Mr. R. Chapman, the treasurer, through business reasons, was compelled to resign, and thus one more of the Old hands retired. A good worker from the inception of the club, his services had been invaluable.

Eventually the following officers were elected, and it is satisfactory to note that they were fairly representative of the town and district :—

President, Mr. Heneage.

Vice-presidents, Earl of Yarborough, Captain Pretyman, Mr. Henri Josse, Mr. J. Wintringham, Mr. T. Hewitt, Mr. A. Bates, Messrs. H. Kelly,

C. F. Carter, R. Cook, F. Osborne, W. G. Marshall, C. M. Mundahl, G. Smith, W. Brocklesby, G. R. Mackerill, T. C. Moss and J. Duke.

Secretary, Mr. I. J. Patmore.

Treasurer, Mr. A. Burnham.

Committee, Messrs. R. C. Hall, C. Maddison, W. Hill, J. Brusey, F. B. Coulson, S. Withers, M. Lawler, W. H. Bellamy and R. Lincoln.

Auditors, Messrs. W. Blanchard and A. H. B. Coulson.

From a casual glance at the above there were some notable additions, some of the officials in the top pews putting their hands down whenever required, whilst a new addition on the Committee was Mr. W. H. Bellamy, but we little thought he was destined to become one of the leading lights in the football world, both on the field and off. Just to give a slight idea of how some of the above assisted the Club, two of us were appointed to visit one of them, H. J., who eventually became a member for the Borough. He resided the other side of Waltham. Of course we were ushered into his presence, and after sampling a little, stated our business. He said "Oh, I understand kicky bally," and to our surprise handed us a cheque good enough for fifty of the best.

With the idea of providing a little of the all necessary it was decided during the close season to hold some old English sports. As they were confined to the members of the football team principally, and were then on professional lines, it was not necessary to obtain any permission to hold them, and they duly came off. Unfortunately the old luck pursued the Directorate and the weather prevented them from being a success from a financial point of view, but otherwise they were not half a bad day's sport. The chief item was the dribbling race round poles. David Black won this with Donald Sutherland second.

Just now a determined effort was being made throughout the country by Messrs. Spalding, the sports providers, of London, to bring the American game of baseball to the front, and with this object in view they gratuitously provided the leading Football Clubs throughout the country with the implements of warfare necessary for the playing of the game. Evidently it must have originated from the old English game of roundy played at every street corner by the youngsters in the old days, but although adopted by the majority of clubs it was anything but a success, and speedily became a sport

of the past. Perhaps it may be interesting to some of the rising generation if
a sketch of it is appended :—

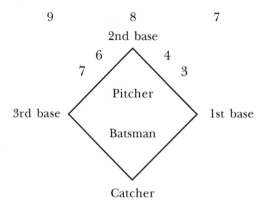

The balls were very similar to lawn tennis balls, but much harder, and
the bat was about 2ft. long, not unlike a policeman's staff.

In comparison to other teams the migration of players from Grimsby
Town was only small, and consisted of McBeth and McKnight. The latter was
missed, but certainly not wanted, as Aston Villa soon found out themselves,
and the consequence was he very soon disappeared from the football world.
With McBeth it was different. For business reasons he returned to Accrington.
We parted the best of friends and are today, in fact Mac often comes over to
see his old pals and also no doubt is pleased to see them, if they call at his
hotel at Sheffield, the Upperthorpe, where he now resides.

Of course it was absolutely necessary that the team should be
strengthened, and Johnny Walker and McNichol and Cosgrove were secured.
Later on local talent was given a chance, neither was it regretted, and the
following quintette were quite good enough for the average team in the
Alliance :

Alf Rose, Hickey Rose, Tom Frith, Charlie Frith, and Murrell.

Considering the financial position of the club, it said much for the
generosity of the Committee that it was decided to give Lundie a benefit.
Great efforts were made to secure a really first-class team, but owing to Cup
Ties and the League, they declined, and ultimately Lincoln City were the
bill of fare. If ever a man deserved a good benefit Jimmy did. He received
about £50, not so bad in the old days, but insignificant in comparison to
some received by the lucky individuals of the present day, the bulk of whom

by no stretch of imagination can be compared to Lundie from a playing point of view.

Certainly one of the biggest body blows from a financial point of view experienced by the club this season, was the refusal of the English Association to elect Grimsby Town in the select eighteen for the competition proper of the English Cup, and, of course, this meant their competing in the qualifying rounds. After due consideration, they decided to slip the Reserves, who went down to Ecclesfield at Sheffield in the first round. Rather annoying, but still it was the correct policy to pursue under the circumstances.

It is useless going into the why and the wherefore of this great injustice. Then and now even, Grimsby Town have never had anything to thank the English Association for, as only last season we had a specimen of it when, after the grand form shown in the Cup Competition, only being beaten by Bradford City, the future winners, away from home, Grimsby Town once more had to fight their way through the qualifying rounds.

As per usual we had some notable outings, some enjoyable, some otherwise. The two most enjoyable were those at Nottingham and Lincoln. Just by way of a change, instead of visiting the Lace Capital in Goose Fair time we went during the Christmas holidays, and after the match adjourned to the Maypole where a dinner and a smoking concert was held, Sam Widdowson in the chair. Now, this was all solid. I plead guilty to being a fairly good judge of these little functions, and you can take it from me that it was indeed a jovial party that departed that night to the fishing metropolis.

It is very satisfactory to note that apparently as far as the Cits and ourselves were concerned better feelings prevailed, with the result that when we arrived at John O'Gaunts we were well received. Quite a novelty. After the match both teams and officials dined together at the Queens, and when Croft with his Gainsborough team called in when they arrived from Derby, things in general were pretty lively. By-the-bye Fred Spikesley, who migrated to Sheffield, one of the best outside lefts England ever had, was amongst the Trinitarians.

During this season several meetings of the Alliance were held. I attended one at Manchester, and brought forward a motion that, if it had come off, would have revolutionized the game. It was to the effect that after this season the League and Alliance adopt a uniform rate of wages, say thirty shillings per week for the Alliance, and three pounds per week for the League. If it had come off, it would have been all right from a Grimbarian point of view, but, of course, it did not suit the wealthier clubs, and it was negatived. On the following morning I joined our team at London Road and accompanied them to Stoke. It was my first visit to the Potteries, and I cannot say I was ever very anxious to repeat it. Their ground is a fine enclosure, in fact one of the best in the Kingdom, but to our surprise we found the charges were 6d., 1s. and 1s. 6d. for grand stand. Quite unusual figures in the old days, but this journey the match was certainly worth it, as it provided the best defensive show ever given in the annals of Grimsby Town. In the second half Stoke were all over our men, but Cob (centre-half), Langley (back) and Ogilvie (goal) gave an exhibition that was quite a revelation to all present. I must acknowledge, to say the least, the opposing forwards had anything but a happy time, and occasionally after Cob and Langley had steadied them Ogilvie would just put his left hand out, and, hey presto, the unfortunate forward would be deposited say about five yards through the goal. This raised the ire of the crowd, and we were precious glad when we had boarded the train en route for Manchester.

As usual arrangements were made for the Christmas Carnival, and amongst the clubs who fixed with us was Woolwich Arsenal, an off-shoot of Notts. Forest. On the very eve they wired that through unforeseen circumstances they could not bring a team. This was indeed hard lines for the Town, and the consequence was that the receipts dropped about £90, a very serious item of course. It never rains but it pours, and we were destined to have a very severe winter, the natural result being that Grimsby Town's finances went down to zero. True, Mr. W. H. Bellamy organized an Archery Tournament, the prizes being given by friends of the Club, but owing to the postponement, through frost, and other causes, only £29 was raised for the funds.

Naturally, just then there was any amount of anxiety concerning the health of the bird in fact he developed so enormously that it was quite on the cards he would follow the example of the frog in Æsop's Fables, and burst, but by judicious attention he survived, but, oh dear, it was a near thing. Just to give you an example of the happy time the executive experienced I will give you an account of a match played at Middlesbrough against the Ironopolis. Thanks to not being in the English Cup Competition we had several vacant dates. One was filled up by accepting the offer of Middlesbrough Ironopolis to visit them, the terms being £40, or half gate if it exceeded £80. I was appointed in charge of the team with a certain prominent trawler owner on the Docks, but how to get there was the problem. It was no good trying to push any more pieces of paper across the mahogany, therefore we visited a well-known chemist in the locality of the Parish Church. Unfortunately he was out, and the only alternative was therefore adopted. Self and brother committee man had to find the needful to pay the fares. This we did, and duly arrived in the Iron Metropolis. Luckily it was a fine day. A good crowd assembled, in fact over £80 was taken at the gate. After the match I went to interview the Secretary, who apparently was a young man of very great importance in his own estimation, and asked him for our share of the gate. Oh, yes, of course, a cheque will be forwarded in due course. I hinted gently that we preferred touching the ready. In a few words he informed me that the idea was absurd, preposterous, &c. For a moment I felt like hurling a few adjectives in a superlative degree at him, but refrained, and laying my hand on his shoulder said, "Young man, have a bit of sense. Are you aware that our team rely on these current coins of the realm for their wages, and therefore it is highly necessary they should be deposited forthwith in these top coat pockets." Eventually he saw the argument, and did the needful. Although surrounded by a great crowd on our journey to the hotel, we were not at all alarmed, the team making a very effective bodyguard.

It may be as well to note that the sequel to this visit was the migration to Middlesbrough of Langley and Jack Taylor and Black. The two former went to Ironopolis, the latter to Middlesbrough. All were good men, and their places took a lot of filling. This caused sundry remarks in the Fisheries, some not very complimentary. Why, I know not, certainly the majority of those making them would have been the very first to accept even a tithe of the amount they received for appending their signatures to the necessary form.

At another meeting of the Alliance, held at Sheffield, Grimsby Town had the satisfaction for the first time in the history of the game, of having a voice on the Committee, I.J.P. being elected. An attempt was also made by us and Sunderland Albion to have the question of paying part fares of visiting teams rectified. The injustice of this was clearly apparent, but it was all in vain, and Sunderland Albion were so wroth that they threatened to resign, which they eventually did.

Notwithstanding our persistent bad luck matches were arranged at the Park with clubs the calibre of Everton, Sunderland and Bolton Wanderers. The two former were lost by a narrow margin, but the latter was drawn. Just now the gates were anything but satisfactory, but we had one bit of luck. The Mayor having declared the day Grimsby became a County Borough as a general holiday, we arranged to play at Abbey Park, and Notts Forest were induced to play their Alliance fixture. Over 4,000 spectators were present — a record for the Park — we won, and the match was a success in every sense of the word.

In the Alliance through the greater part of the season the form shown had been anything but satisfactory, in a great measure attributable to the absolute indifference shown by a section of the team as to whether the matches were won or not. This necessitated a little straight talking, and the result was that Grimsby Town came with a rush at the termination of the season, in fact 17 points were secured out of the last 18 — a brilliant performance, one also that put us once more in a prominent position when the table was cast up.

At the termination of the season the performances of the team were not at all unsatisfactory, especially considering they had a railway journey for their Alliance matches of an average distance of 222 miles, all made the same day, and met teams the calibre of Everton, Sunderland, and Bolton Wanderers in the ordinary fixtures. Here they are :—

ALLIANCE.

Matches				Goals		
Played	Won	Drawn	Lost	For	Against	Points
22	11	5	6	43	26	28

ALL MATCHES.

42	21	15	6	30	64

To the bulk of the well wishers of the Town it was evident that the period had arrived in the history of the Club when it must either be disbanded or, as an alternative, be formed into a Limited Liability Company. Through various causes which I have mentioned, we were, roughly speaking, practically some £500 to the bad, and with the prospect of other expenses looming in the future it was scarcely fair that we unfortunate owners of the bird should incur further liabilities. With this object in view a special meeting was held. It was recommended to the general meeting shortly to be held that the club be formed into a Limited Liability Company of £1,500 capital in £1 shares, 5s. to be paid on application, 2s. 6d. on allotment, and 2s. 6d. in August.

The most critical meeting ever held by Grimsby Town duly came off. After considerable discussion the balance-sheet was passed, it being pointed out that we had a certain amount of assets on the ground, it having cost £300 making, but unfortunately as it was only on a short lease too much importance could not be attached to this. After this the most important business on the agenda was whether the club should become a Limited Liability one or not. It was pointed out by the Secretary that all the Football Clubs that had been enrolled as Limited Companies had not adopted exactly the same policy. For instance some were guaranteed 5s. per cent. dividend on their shares, whereas others agreed to allow the profits to go to the club. Eventually it was carried to form the Club into a Limited Liability Company, and a powerful directorate was elected. The capital was to be £1,500 in £1 shares with other details as recommended by the special meeting, with the proviso that all profits in the matter of dividends were to go to the club. Before the meeting terminated the Chairman suggested that a large amount of the capital might he raised through the working-men supporters of the Club taking one share each. This was very good in theory, but unfortunately it did not come out very well in practice.

For several reasons, not above a score took shares, some blaming the articles which alloted all profits to the benefit of the Club, but in my opinion this was not all the cause, the simple fact being that they emphatically objected to buy the bird, or in other words, pay the debts of those unfortunates on the Committee, who by gross mismanagement, as several were kind enough to say, had incurred them. Rough, wasn't it ? But it was ever thus, nor will it alter in the future. It is simply a species of human nature.

Of course there is no denying the soft impeachment that if the required capital had been subscribed, the existing debts would have been discharged. This followed as a matter of course, but it is nevertheless a fact that some followers of the game were so ignorant as to think the guarantees had no

security. True, the value did not cover their liability, but still considering they held the lease of the land, and also had control of the ground appointments it was evident they held in common parlance the trump card.

Unfortunately instead of the 1,500 shares beiing subscribed, about 400 were applied for, and not a few of these were never fully paid up. Naturally it was absolutely impossible to continue on these lines, but certain arrangements were made between the owners of the bird and the Directorate of the New Company now registered.

On the formation of the Company, of course, all of us that enjoyed the position of guarantors — I don't think — resigned, but to safeguard their interests, it was arranged that bills should be floated to meet the old liabilities to cover a period of no less than five years, in fact, ten of six months, and by this means alone was it possible for Grimsby Town to continue.

Just by way of a change the English Association once more made us go through the Qualifying Rounds, a great injustice, but still this season we had not got the Alliance fixtures made, and therefore it was decided to leave dates vacant.

Some time since I remarked that our relations with Lincoln City had much improved, in fact we had become quite friendly, and the result was that principally through our efforts they were admitted to the Alliance. It was, however, only after a great struggle, as after tieing on the first Council, they got in by a majority of one. This season the Alliance consisted of the following clubs :— Sheffield Wednesday, Bootle, Newton Heath, Walsall, Notts. Forest, Burton Swifts, Lincoln City, Small Heath Alliance, Crewe Alexander, Ardwick, Birmingham St. George's, Grimsby Town.

One little item that seriously affected the prospects of the English Clubs was the policy adopted by the Scottish Association of reinstating the innocents abroad, who had wandered across the border, and had played for English clubs, for an inducement shall we say. Yes, the olive branch was offered them. They were reinstated as full blown amateurs. Better have put them in some museum, as clearly they were the great novelty of the day, viz., a Scotsman refusing the almighty dollar.

At the commencement of this season a lot of ill feeling was knocking about amongst some of the old season ticket-holders, as by the new rule adopted, only shareholders were granted the privilege of having season tickets at a reduced figure, viz., 10s., but, of course, tickets were still obtainable by any person for the reserved portion of the stand, at £1 1s 0d.

With the near approach of Season 1891-2, strong efforts were made to secure some capable players to strengthen the team, and Gray, who played for Aston Villa, Ackroyd, G. McBeth, and Devlin, and later on Elliman, an Irish International were secured. By no stretch of the imagination could they be compared to the captures of preceding years, in fact, with the exception of Gray, who was a good man, and possibly Ackroyd, better local talent existed at home, as was clearly proved ere the season finished.

If for nothing else this season was noticeable for the passing of the rule re penalty kick, and not before time. As you know, even amongst the leading teams, not the slightest hesitation was shown in tripping a man, and they were not very particular how they did it either. Naturally it had a good effect on the game, and it is rather singular to note at this period it invariably resulted in a goal. Why they should be so frequently missed now is indeed a problem.

This season the Directorate decided if possible to work their way through the qualifying rounds of the competition proper. The first two rounds came off all right, but in the third round they met admittedly the strongest team in the Division, viz., Sheffield United. Luckily, however, they were drawn at home. The Sheffielders at once opened negotiations to have the match played at Sheffield, offering a guarantee of £100, and half the gate over £200. The Directorate of the Town, however, refused this, asking £200, or half gate over £400, not that they had any idea that it would be given. They rather preferred playing at home, as there was more than a chance of winning. The result was that Sheffield United relieved Grimsby Town of any further anxiety re the destination of the English Cup.

It is rather singular that just prior to this match when they appeared for Adam Ogilvie's benefit, they were beaten. Adam, however, received a substantial sum, and who will say he did not deserve it, for never a straighter man kicked a football.

Just by way of a change, the form shown by the team the greater portion of this season was wretched in the extreme, in fact, we figured ignominiously at the bottom of the Alliance Table. Form like this was of course too bad to be true, and eventually improved somewhat but too late to retrieve our reputation. Various causes were advanced as to the reason of it, but probably one true cause was the laxity of the employment system. In these days employment as labourers was found for the bulk of the imported ones. Unfortunately they did not know what a good thing was, and took advantage of it. What it cost some of the tradesmen would be a veritable eye opener to the majority of the people that condescend to wade through these pages, one, in fact, told me that he estimated the loss at £1 per week during the football season.

Another item indulged in by a few of the team was the insuring of themselves against accidents, and they made the pace so hot that the Insurance Companies had had quite sufficient of it the very first season. Here is a sample. Just on the eve of a very important match I happened to go down to the ground to see them practice, when, to my surprise, a very prominent member of the team was sat in the grand stand. Naturally I had a word with him, and he informed me that he had a severe pain in his inside. Of course I had no means of proving otherwise, but going down Freeman Street the same afternoon I met the local agent of the Insurance Company. Casually I introduced the insurance question, and to my surprise he informed me that he had been notified by the very player I had been talking to to the effect that he had happened an accident and hurt his ankle, and would he see to the matter at once. Instead I did, telling the aforesaid agent I was not an authority on anatomy, but l was not aware the ankle was situated in the belly, and if the player did not turn out on Saturday, he would hear further about it. It is satisfactory to note that he did, and played well, too. The idea was all right if it had come off, wasn't it?

For some time the feeling had been prevalent that an attempt should be made across the water to establish an Association Club on a firm basis. Negotiations were opened, and the result was that Everton and Grimsby Town met to give an exhibition game, but it was all in vain, although a good crowd assembled, and seemed delighted by the form shown. Rugby football, however, was just then in the zenith of its power, and the experiment was doomed to be a failure from the first.

Just at this period of the game possibly the favourite referee of the day was Fitzroy Norris, and not without reason. Of spare build, and tall, he was in the pink of condition, and was quite capable of following the play throughout the game. To give some idea of how his services were appreciated, he travelled no less than 5,460 miles to fulfil his duties, a record in the old days.

Just now the position of Grimsby Town in the Football World was critical in the extreme. Apparently we had no chance of getting away from the last four in the Alliance table. The result was that the bird was seriously ill, and the Directorate had many an anxious hour in the Committee-room. Of course the probability was that we might be re-elected, but there were any amount of applicants ready for the position, and there was a strong feeling against us in the Midlands especially. Luckily for us, however, there was such a multiplicity of schemes brought to the front that we were enabled to work our points very well. After all it was only by a great injustice we did not finish sixth in the Alliance. Simply through having two points deducted for playing McUrick against Crewe Alexandra, and our form in all matches was also not so bad. Here it is :—

Matches				Goals	
Played	Won	Drawn	Lost	For	Against
44	16	12	8	105	81

However, it was thought better to draw a table out ot the nine clubs that had been in the Alliance since its inception. Here it is :—

	Matches				Goals		
	Played	Won	Lost	Drawn	For	Against	Pts.
Notts. Forest	66	29	21	16	155	122	74
Sheffield W.	66	31	24	11	174	139	73
Grimsby Town	66	29	27	10	141	114	68
Newton Heath	66	28	26	12	246	133	68
Small Heath	66	25	29	12	152	163	62
Crewe Alexandra	66	26	30	10	170	175	62
Bootle	66	24	31	11	148	164	59
Birmingham St. George's	66	26	34	6	161	175	58
Walsall Town	66	23	34	9	111	169	55

Acasual glance will show that we occupied the third position by goal average, also that the results proved we had the strongest defence in the Alliance. This table proved very useful. In fact it was the means of our continuing in the football world. Just now there was any amount of bad feeling between the Leagues, especially in the North, and a meeting was called between the Northern League and the Alliance, the idea being to amalgamate, admitting a few clubs like Sheffield Wednesday, &c., and forming a powerful League of 38 clubs. Once more train fares wrecked it, or were the indirect cause of it, as it was decided to run it in three divisions,

No. 1 .... 16 clubs
No. 2 .... 12 clubs
No. 3 .... 10 clubs

This, of course, was obviously unfair and naturally the scheme became a thing of the past, but to our great delight at a meeting held in Sheffield it was decided to form a league consisting of two divisions, the first of sixteen clubs and the second of twelve, and we were selected members of the Second Division. When the question of promotion or otherwise came on the carpet the following remarkable propositions were agreed upon :—

I.   That the bottom three in the First Division play the top three in the Second Division for the right of retaining their positions :—

No. 16   Division 1 playing   No. 1   Division 2
No. 15   Division 1 playing   No. 2   Division 2
No. 14   Division 1 playing   No. 3   Division 2

A very absurd resolution never likely to be at all workable, as indeed it proved at the termination of the season.

The second, of course, was quite in order only instead of the bottom two having to retire as in the present day, no less than four teams had to face the music.

Having secured a new lease of life, at least in a playing point of view, determined efforts were made by the Directorate to improve the financial position of the club, and every assistance was given by the old guarantors, to which I had the doubtful honour to belong, inasmuch as we did not press our claims. Amongst the various ideas mooted was the holding of a series of dances and smoking-concerts at the Masonic Hall, and an archery tournament on a larger scale than usual. A tremendous amount of work was put in by all concerned, especially by the Hon. Secretaries, Messrs. Chris. White and W. H. Bellamy, but it is very satisfactory to note that by their efforts and a benefit given by Mr. H. J. Curry at the Prince of Wales Theatre no less than £195 6s. 8d. was added to the revenue of the Club.

This season, just by way of a change, although Fairley and Mullen, centre forward of Paisley Street, Mirren, were secured from across the border it was decided to angle in other waters, and the Birmingham district was tried, the result being the signing on of Higgins, Whitehouse and Fletcher for a mere song. What a trio! As anyone of the old school knows Higgins developed into a grand all-round player. Whitehouse was certainly the best man Grimsby Town ever had between the sticks, whilst Harry Fletcher, now in business in Albert Street, was a veritable pocket Hercules; brilliant and tricky to a degree, he was the means years afterwards when we transferred him to Notts. County of keeping them in the First Division, and even today, eighteen years after, is capable of playing a game quite good enough for a Midland League team.

This season Davie Riddoch was entitled to a benefit, and therefore arrangements were made with our dear friends, the Cits., to oblige us with a fixture at Abbey Park. It duly came off. A good crowd assembled, and the Directorate were enabled to hand over to Davie a substantial sum of money as benefits went in the old days.

This season it was decided to make a determined effort in the English Cup Competition. Having beaten Attercliffe in the First Round we were drawn against Doncaster Rovers away in the Second. Little did we think what a struggle we should have with them ere we dismissed them from the Competition. At the first attempt, although we had much the better of the game, we were extremely lucky to draw, as they rushed a goal through on time. Candidly, the majority of us thought we had lost, but to our delight, for some technical point or other, it was disallowed. They lodged an objection, and the Association ordered the match to be replayed at Doncaster. With a good crowd we duly appeared and after a desperate struggle won, but not without Tom Frith having a leg broken. After the match the crowd indulged in the doubtful pastime of stoning our team. Jimme Lundie was the unwilling recipient of one of these missiles, and just then would very much have liked to have had an interview with the thrower of the same.

In the Third Round we obliged Gainsborough Trinity with the order of the knock, whilst in the fourth we condescended to once more relieve our dear friends, the Cits, from any further anxiety re the destination of the Cup for the current season, but only after a desperate struggle, as the latter thought it just about time they made a determined effort to break the record by at length winning an English Cup Tie against Grimsby Town.

Having reached the competition proper once more, Stockton were our next victims, not half either, as they were beaten five to nil, but the visit to Darwen in the Second Round was a bird of quite a different feather. In these days the latter club was very strong, one of the best in Lancashire, and besides had a very peculiar ground, so it was not altogether surprising that at length we were defeated. After the match, as usual, we went on to Manchester, and spent the night there, and a jolly good time we had, let me tell you.

It may be interesting to note that the gate money in the competition proper was £65 in the Stockton match and £85 in the Darwen match. It scarcely requires a Solomon to see that after all the expenses, etc., had been taken out there was precious little left to pay the wages of the team, in fact, seven Cup Ties this season in the English Cup were a dead loss from a pecuniary point of view, a matter much to be regretted.

As usual, we partook of a little Scotch at Christmas time, the Royal Scots from York, and Cambuslang, a Glasgow team, who came with a big reputation, being the bill of fare. Neither team was above the ordinary and as usual got beaten, but possibly the most disappointing item was that the latter team had no players good enough for us to induce to stay in the Fisheries.

For some time it had become fashionable to play matches at night by the aid of Wells lights. Personally I could never see anything attractive in them, without it was the weird appearance players and officials appeared to have on the field of play. This season we were invited to play a match with Sheffield United at Hull for the benefit of the Hull medical charities. It duly came off, a tremendous crowd assembled. We lost, but this was quite immaterial, as our object was obtained, inasmuch as the exchequer of the charities received a substantial increase by our efforts in conjunction with Sheffield United.

Considering how near we are and the facilities we possess of getting across to Holland, Germany, etc., it is nothing short of remarkable that Grimsby Town have never sent a team across. This season the suggestion was mooted, but it did not come off. If it had Grimsby Town would have been about the first club of note to introduce the "Soccer" code abroad.

As everybody knows, since Grimsby Town has been a club, Good Friday and Saturday have always been looked upon as red letter days from a financial point of view, and this proved to be no exception to the rule. With Sheffield United and Walsall Town, two League fixtures, records were expected to be made, and so they were, especially in the former match, £102 being taken at the gate. Such a sum as this appears absurd in modern football, and therefore little doubt need be felt that just now the financing of a football club was not a joy for ever.

It goes without saying that in the first year of its inception the League was a grand success to both divisions. It took any amount of anxiety from the various officials, by absolutely securing a good list of fixtures. In fact with Cup Ties the card was full, and also in some cases it was the means of attracting gates large enough to meet the current expenses of a few of the clubs, and it was a few indeed. As a matter of fact it was an open secret that there were only about three clubs solvent, Everton, Sheffield Wednesday and Bolton Wanderers. This fact being recognised, J.J.B., a great authority on the game of this period, toured the country with the idea of inducing the various directorates to agree to a reduction of the wage list, but in vain, and the result was that clubs were continually on the verge of bankruptcy.

When the figures were cast up in the League it was found that Sunderland headed the First Division with 30 matches and 48 points, whilst Small Heath enjoyed that distinction in the Second Division with 22 matches and 36 points. Grimsby Town did well, finishing fourth, just missing the test matches, with the following record :—

Matches				Goals		
Played	Won	Drawn	Lost	For	Against	Points
22	11	10	1	42	41	23

On the other hand Lincoln City were in the cart, or, in other words, were in the last four, requiring re-election. When the playing off was the order of the day the absurdity of it was at once apparent, inasmuch as it was proved conclusively that whereas it was possible for the club No. 14 in the First Division to lose its position No. 16 might retain theirs. Clearly it was ridiculous, and a very sensible resolution was decided on, viz., to increase the Second Division to sixteen clubs by electing Rotherham Town, Newcastle United, Royal Arsenal and Liverpool. This was a rare piece of luck for the City as it was nearly a certainty they would not have been re-elected owing to the latter clubs having so much influence at headquarters. When the general meeting was held it could easily be seen that financially at all events the club was in a very bad way, and no wonder, for instead of the £1,500 being taken up in scrip, only £474 had been applied for, and even all these had not been fully paid up, in fact only £361 11s. had been received. Naturally just now the bird was very bad indeed and although he received the very best of attention apparently he was on the verge of collapsing. Where there is life, however, there is always hope, and so it appeared in this instance, as the guarantors, ever willing to assist the club, came to a certain arrangement (destined to become an accomplished fact before long) by which his life was prolonged, but how near Grimsby Town was just now of having Ichabod written over its tombstone was only known by a select few.

Considering it was in this position it was nothing short of astounding that not a few of the general public had an idea that it was a good thing to be on the directorate and enjoy the good things knocking about. One in particular was very anxious, and we obliged him by getting him on. It did not take him long to learn something of the inner mysteries of financing a football team. In fact he was speedily relieved of about £20 and gracefully retired a sadder but wiser man.

SEASON 1893-4.

It says much to the credit of the Directorate that ere the season commenced a determined effort was made to get rid of the old incubus that hung round the neck of the Club, the idea being to get fifty guarantors of £15 each. About thirty were easily found, alas it was principally the old crowd, but it was ever thus. It is the easiest thing in the world to talk. Birds of this description are easily found, but it is slightly different to find one that is willing to put his hand down, indeed a rara avis. As usual the search for him was a failure, and the arrangement previously alluded to appeared more a certainty than ever.

Evidently Grimsby Town just now had a good name. There were any amount of attempts to poach in their preserves, some, it must be acknowledged, with a certain amount of success. As a result the following figured in the ranks of the leading clubs :—

Everton, F. Geary and J. Walker.

Wolverhampton, D. Black.

Blackburn R., A. Ogilvie.

Sheffield W., A. Langley.

Sheffield U., C. H. Howlett.

As usual it was necessary to have the angling apparatus out, and a fairly good catch was the result of the operations. The following arrived in the Fisheries :— Graham, Crawford, Russell, Jones and McCairns. Of these Crawford was the failure, the others were more than useful. Indeed McCairns on his day was brilliant, and also was one of the greatest favourites that ever toed a ball in the Fisheries.

This season Ackroyd had his benefit, a strong contingent of Notts. Forest players coming down for the occasion. Little interest was taken in the match, but all the same Ackroyd had a fairly substantial sum to touch at the finish.

At Christmas time two good matches were down for decision at the Park, viz., our old friends, Royal Scots and Royal Arsenal (who even now were not known as Woolwich Arsenal). Such was the desperate position of Grimsby Town from a financial point of view (oh, that bird) that an appeal was made to the shareholders and ticket holders to waive their claim for free admission and pay at the gate like ordinary people. This journey it is a pleasure to note that practically to a man they did the needful, and just for once the treasurer was seen to wear a double-six smile.

If for nothing else this season proved that once more Grimsby Town were qualified to beat anything in our division in the Qualifying Round. A team rejoicing in the name of Wath-on-Dearne were our first victims, our dear friends, the Cits., were the second just by way of a change, the third was Grantham Rovers and the fourth Gainsborough Trinity. This, as usual, landed us in the competition proper once more, and we were lucky enough to be drawn against Liverpool at home. Naturally, this caused any amount of excitement, the leading item being that it leaked out by some means or other that Liverpool had made us an offer to play the match on the West Coast instead of the East. This was quite true. Several of their Directors met ours, but it was only after a long debate in which the points were fairly considered that we consented to waive our right of grounds for a good substantial sum, £200 in fact, and half gate if it exceeded £400.

Left to Right—J. Shepherd, J. Whitehouse, W. Lindsey, T. Stott, W. H. Bellamy, H. Higgins, A. Murrel, T. Frith, W. Allen, T. McCormack, top row.

H. Rose, J. Graham, D. Riddock, middle row.

Photo by] J. Murray, G. Eccleston, T. McCairns, H. Fletcher, T. Pratt. [R. Wilson, Hull.

GRIMSBY TOWN F.C., 1894-5.

91

Of course, amongst the well wishers of the Club, I don't think this caused any amount of criticism, but it was properly treated by those at the helm with contempt, and well it might, as, after the expenses incurred by fighting our way through the Qualifying Rounds it was absolutely necessary to make a substantial sum out of the competition proper if Grimsby Town Football Club was to keep on the map.

After the excitement had subsided the necessary arrangements were made with the Great Central Rajlway to run an excursion to suit the Pontoonites. Nine o'clock was fixed for the time of departure, the team going over night. When the day arrived our usual party was formed in the saloon, amongst whom was a cousin of Councillor Dick J., from San Francisco. From the first everything went wrong, commencing with the engine. To say the least his remarks were caustic, and we had the pleasure of hearing his opinion on our railways. When we arrived at Sheffield it had been arranged to have a substantial lunch put in the saloon. The supposed lunch duly arrived. I took one detachment with the idea that it represented the menu for yours truly. Imagine my surprise when I was informed, courteously enough I will admit, that it was for three persons. After a few remarks of mine as to whether they were catering for a few decayed missionaries we had to accept the inevitable.

After all, however, this was not the only disappointment experienced at Sheffield. One of our comrades was missing, Hugh Todd, as grand a specimen of the Scottish Race as ever crossed the border. This caused quite a gloom amongst a section of us, personal friends of his, as we were quite certain something out of the ordinary had occurred or he would have been with us. The result was that a prepaid wire was sent to his lodgings, the reply to be sent to the Neptune Hotel, Liverpool. As a climax to this miserable journey we arrived at Liverpool too late. As a matter of fact although we took cabs the teams were well on with the second half. A bit rough, wasn't it, after the long journey from East to West.

After the match a cab was taken to the Neptune by yours truly, Dick C., Tommy L., and Bill C., &c., and never shall I forget the shock we received when the fatal wire was opened stating that poor Hugh had been drowned the previous night in the Humber in his attempt to board the boat for New Holland. It was indeed a body blow, and we all required a steadier or two ere we recovered from the shock. Handing half a dollar for one of these steadiers to my surprise another 3d. was required, a very exorbitant charge. After this I said we had better have our tea here. A casual glance convinced me there was no danger of a second Sheffield disaster. We duly sat down. I felt in form. After about half-an-hour the waiter started to load me with any amount of brawn. At last I could not stand it any longer, and asked where all the spotted granite came from, whether Schulke came that way. He smiled, so did I, and when I arose you can take it from me they had not paid the rent out of our visit. It is scarcely necessary to mention that on the journey home a gloom settled throughout the excursion, and when the body of poor Hugh Todd was found it was a sorrowful party which journeyed to the New Cemetery, where a stone was erected on the grave of one of the best and truest comrades that ever crossed the border.

After our dismissal from the English Cup attention was directed to the League, and a veritable bom-shell fell on the football world, inasmuch as Bootle announced that owing to financial reasons they were compelled to retire from the League. This, to those in the know, was not at all surprising. The fact was that Liverpool had the money, and therefore the team, and Bootle as a consequence were outclassed in every respect. It is very remarkable that the retirement of Bootle from the League was the indirect cause of a veritable eye-opener in the football world, at least as far as Grimsby was concerned. To fill the vacant date a match was arranged between the Town League team and the All Saints, the leading junior team of the town. To everybody's surprise it resulted in a tie, indeed the Saints led the greater portion of the game. This match was talked about years after, indeed it was mentioned to me quite recently, the general idea being that the Town slipped the Reserves. To prove otherwise I append the teams, and it will readily be seen that the teams were at full strength.

GRIMSBY TOWN.

Whitehouse; Lundie and T. Frith; Higgins, Graham and Russell; A. Rose, Fletcher, McCairns, Ackroyd and Jones.

ALL SAINTS.

Bagshaw; Murrel and Walker; Pegg, Walton and Hall; Smith, Middleton, Dore, Hollingsworth and Taylor.

Referee, Albert H. Coulson.

Even after this performance it was simply marvellous the apathy with which junior football was treated. The public absolutely refused to patronise them, and the result was they simply existed by being strictly amateur and having the assistance of friends, genuine sportsmen, who were not above putting their hands down when it was necessary. Whilst on the subject of local talent, I cannot let this opportunity pass without a word or two on the subtect. Then, as now, the prejudice was great against it, and yet we had men the calibre of H. Smith (Cob), Houltby, Hopewell, the three Friths (Tom, Charlie and Wink), Murrel, Alf and Hickey Rose, Bagshaw, J. Taylor, and others I could mention, who, when the opportunity occurred, showed form infinitely superior to many a party playing for Grimsby Town that had the magic word Mac in front of his name, a sure recommendation in the old days.

At the termination of the season it was an open secret that Grimsby Town was in a bad way financially, and our friends at Nottingham very kindly offered to bring a team to play a match for the funds of the Club. Here was an opportunity for the supporters of the Club. The match was well advertised. It duly took place, and about 300 spectators were present. Comment is unnecessary.

When the League tables were finally cast up this journey Aston Villa headed the First League with the following record: Matches played 30, points 44. In the Second Division Liverpool sported the flag — matches 28, points 48. It is satisfactory to note that Grimsby Town did not do at all badly, indeed they finished fifth, just outside the Qualifying Rounds once more. Here is the record

Matches				Goals		
Played	Won	Drawn	Lost	For	Against	Points
28	15	 11	 2	 71	57	 32

At the termination of the season the Football League held one of the most important meetings ever held. It was a well-known fact that a certain amount of jealousy existed between the First and Second Divisions and deliberate attempts were made by the First League to practically crush the Second by increasing the first to 20 clubs and reducing the second to 14. The latter had, however, a strong weapon in their hands, as by voting solid it was impossible for the first to obtain a three-fourths majority, and the consequence was that the little plot failed.

It is interesting to note that at this meeting Lincolnshire at last had another representative elected. Ever since Mr. Patmore resigned we were quite unrepresented, therefore were delighted when my old friend, John Henry Strawson, of Lincoln City fame, was elected. It is remarkable that although W. H. Bellamy was comparatively new to the football world he made such an impression on those present that he was within an ace of being elected, in fact he was only two short.

For some time the Cits. had claimed that they were the premier team of the County. On what grounds was somewhat of a problem. This season we once more had waded our way in the Competition, and in fact had repeated it several times before any other Lincolnshire teams figured in the list, but the greatest argument against the claims of the Cits. was the astounding fact that they had never once beaten us in an English Cup Tie. Indeed the sequence of wins of Grimsby Town was remarkable. Whether at home or away, the Cits. were beaten, an operation, mind you, highly necessary for us to get amongst the top sawyers of the football world.

SEASON 1894-5.

When the general meeting was held the fate of the Club hung in the balance, as, whatever their prospects from a playing point of view, the time had clearly come when it was absolutely necessary that some definite understanding should be arrived at re the old debt, or as an alternative the Club should be disbanded. Ever willing to assist the Club, the old guarantors, some of whom, including myself, had retired from the board when it was formed into a Limited Company, made an offer, which I think you will admit showed they had still an interest in the welfare of the Club, on certain conditions, viz., that they would meet two of the bills long overdue, which had been repeatedly renewed, the amount being £113 6s. The offer was accepted, cheques were signed by each of us for a proportion of the amount, and the bills were duly met. That grand all round sportsman, the late F. B. Coulson, by some means or other, secured the original Round Robins and had them framed.

It was understood that the all necessary should be refunded to us, but alas, that day never arrived, neither did we expect it, as we were all quite

Herbert E. Speechley,

Decorator,

Grimsby and Cleethorpes.

Designs, Sketches and Specifications

Prepared for all kinds of Decorations,

Villas, Public Buildings, Churches,

Chapels, etc.

BUSINESS PREMISES :—

SEA VIEW STREET, CLEETHORPES.

HAINTON AVENUE & BRADLEY STREET,

GRIMSBY.

willing to sacrifice the amount to save the Club from being a relic of the past.

The atmosphere being somewhat cleared the Chairman and Directorate, although faced with a deficit of some £393 4s. 3d., old account, fondly hoped that the shareholders at least who had not fully paid up their script would do so, the precise amount being £97 3s. Then by adding a little to it, two more bills could be met and possibly the remainder by the current revenue of the ensuing season. Alas, as usual, they were doomed to disappointment, the result being that the bird, although amputated, still lingered. After all, there was one satisfactory motion carried at the meeting, viz., the proposition to have a small committee of five elected, to be known as the Team Management Committee. This was a step in the right direction, and with one of the best trainers of today, Billy Allen, on the ground staff, everything pointed to a capital season, from a playing point of view at all events.

This season the charges for admission were revised, and the following scale adopted :— Boys, 5s. 6d.; ladies, 7s. 6d.; gentlemen, 10s. 6d.; ladies and gentlemen, one guinea; subscribers, one guinea; the last two having the use of the reserved portion of the covered stand.

Naturally the team required strengthening, and with this object in view the following players were duly landed :— Lindsey (Everton), Waterstone (Arbroath), Stott (Liverpool), Frost (Middlesbrough), Eccleston (Brum District), Whitehouse (Army), Murray (Dundee). Bar Whitehouse, although severely tested during the season, they proved quite up to the average, Lindsey, Stott, and Eccleston, being possibly the best.

Thanks to the new rule re transfer, the Town received a welcome addition to their exchequer in the shape of a cheque for ten guineas from the Bolton Wanderers for the transfer of Henderson. Unfortunately through Dan Doyle not staying with them any length of time we received nothing for him. By-the-bye, I wonder how much Grimsby Town would want now for the transfer of a back the calibre of Dan Doyle.

Of course, different ideas were afloat to raise a certain amount of money to meet current expenses, and for the first and only time a grand sacred concert was held at the Park. The Temperance Band of Barton provided a bill of fare. A collection was taken at the gate. It was not a success, neither did it deserve to be.

Just now from a playing point of view everything pointed well, the Team were showing grand form. Here's a specimen. Four matches away in twelve days against Walsall, Newcastle, Woolwich, and Barton, the distance averaging 262 miles per match. Considering they had not the facilities for travelling they have now, the following record will bear inspection :—

Matches				Goals		
Played	Won	Drawn	Lost	For	Against	Points
4	2	2	0	10	7	4

Although I had not always the pleasure of travelling with the Team I have a vivid recollection of being linesman at Hyde Road grounds, Manchester, where we played Manchester City. The latter were the re-organised Ardwick Club, had got a strong team together, and expected to fairly pulverize our team. Unfortunately for them on our arrival an old Grimbarian, Mr. W. Morley, then living in Manchester, met us, and promptly promised the Team a new hat each if they won. George Mitchell, the only director present, likewise promised a supper. Whether this was the cause of it I am not aware, but from the first our team played like demons, and to the surprise of a big crowd won the match by five goals to two. After the match in a conversation with Mr. Parlby, their secretary, an old friend I had frequently met at Committees, &c., he informed me that although his club did not recognise the debts of the defunct Ardwick, they nevertheless had decided to send Grimsby Town a cheque for fifty shillings in settlement of the old debt that had been in dispute for some years, so altogether Grimsby Town had a good day, both from a playing and pecuniary point of view.

In the English Cup Competition we once more obliged the Cits., then Attercliffe, but the Third Round against Worksop was a regular cough drop. When they were first drawn to play at the Park, from a betting point of view I dare say the odds would have been at least 100 to one against them, and therefore you can imagine our surprise, not to say consternation, when by about the biggest fluke on record they secured a goal practically in the dark and relieved us of any further anxiety for the present year. This, however, in more senses than one, was looked upon as a blessing, as just then we occupied a good position in the League, and with ordinary luck stood a good chance of getting into the test matches, a sure source of revenue, and through them possibly into the First League. Unfortunately we soon had an experience which convinced us that to achieve our object we should have to do something out of the ordinary. I allude to the match with Notts. County, the winners of the English Cup last season. When they appeared at the Park we led at half-time by three goals to two, and they not only had to face a gale of wind but likewise were a man short, so everything pointed to our winning easily, but to everybody's surprise, the umpire, a Burnley man, decided the ground was unfit for play, a gross injustice to Grimsby Town. In the replay Notts. won one to nil, which made all the difference when the table was finally cast up.

Fortunately, we were not without friends this season, one of whom was the Railway Company, who offered us every facility in the home matches, bringing us home sometimes coupled on to a coal train so that hotel expenses were saved. Here's a specimen. I have known us leave the Black Country say at five o'clock, travel via Manchester, eventually landing at Wakefield at 11 o'clock in time to catch an excursion home, arriving at two a.m. This was not the only favour granted us this season, inasmuch as they relieved us of any liability re our trips to Attercliffe and Lincoln City, ordinary matches, which were failures, and likewise ran excursions from Frodingham, etc., to enable people to patronize our matches at a nominal cost.

Possibly the Easter Monday League Match at Leicester was one of the most important matches ever played by Grimsby Town, as on the result it depended whether Grimsby Town were in the test matches or not. Of course, an excursion was run, about 1,000 making the journey. When we arrived at the Walnut Street ground there were at least 10,000 present, and after a desperate struggle they beat us. It was naturally a great disappointment to us to once more get on the very threshold, as it were, only to be beaten in the last lap. After tea the majority of us rushed to the station to catch the ordinary to Nottingham so that we could spend yet another night at the Maypole. Ere this came off some of us were destined to have quite an adventure. Here it is. Three of our Directors, a farmer of Scartho and myself, had got into the train in a compartment next to the engine and comfortably seated when a porter, a fussy individual, coming to us promptly ordered us out. If he had been civil we might have obliged, but he wasn't and one of the Directors started arguing the point with him. To the Director's great surprise the porter seized him roughly by the collar and dragged him on the platform. Result:

Arrival of the Stationmaster. The Director duly reported the porter and the stationmaster asking what the porter did, I thought it the better plan to give him a practical illustration, and seizing the aforesaid porter — he was only little, mind you — by the neck, shook him nicely. By some means or other his head bumped occasionally on the shutters of Smith's stall. This more than satisfied the stationmaster, as he threatened to call the police, but after he found out that we were amongst the guarantors of the excursion he quite altered his tune, and advised the porter to be more careful in future. When we arrived at Nottingham the adventure oozed out, and it was illustrated at the expense of one brother scribe, E. C. T., who scarcely saw the joke.

During the season a capital list of ordinary matches were arranged, amongst them being the visit of the Blackburn Rovers, with Ogilvie in goal. They appeared at full strength, with a team nearly good enough to win the English Cup, but taking things somewhat easily perhaps at first, found they had run against a team distinctly above the average. But their effort was too late. The Town were in full song, and, despite the grand form shown by Adam in goal the Rovers were beaten by four goals to nil, and on that day's play they were certainly the inferior team. This season the Town finished fifth in the League, the position of the first five clubs being as follows :—

	Matches				Goals		
	Played	Won	Lost	Drawn	For	against	Pts.
Bury	30	23	5	2	78	33	48
Notts	30	17	8	5	75	45	39
Newton Heath	30	15	7	8	78	44	38
Leicester Fosse	30	15	7	8	72	53	38
Grimsby Town	30	18	11	1	79	52	37

A casual glance will convince any unbiassed person that this season at all events we were robbed of test match honours by the injustice done us in the Rotherham and Notts. matches, as with four additional points we should have finished second, and with two points third.

1895-6.

In the close season a very important meeting of the Football League was held, at which the much ventilated question of the unsatisfactory methods adopted in the test matches was one of the leading items. Eventually it was decided that only the two bottom teams of the First Division and the two top teams in the Second Division should meet in the test matches and play home and home fixtures. This obviously was an improvement, but still it was not a satisfactory solution to the difficulty, neither was one found until the present one was adopted, namely compulsory retirement of the bottom clubs.

One satisfactory item of the meeting was the election of Mr. W. H. Bellamy on the Committee instead of Mr. J. H. Strawson, of the Cits., which, of course, gave Grimsby Town once more a direct voice in the management of the League, a very important item to Grimsby Town. How he continued to serve on this important Committee with credit to himself is now a matter of history, and it goes without saying he was the means of doing Grimsby Town many a good turn in the football world.

When the general meeting was held a better tone prevailed among the members assembled, for had not the guarantors come to the rescue to a certain extent, but the bird still existed, mutilated it is true, and the Directorate made a direct appeal to the members to make the bazaar to be held in December a great success, and thus find the all necessary to pay the incubus off that had crippled Grimsby Town for so many years.

Just now the Town were feeling the benefits of the transfer system and Preston North End obliged them by sending on a cheque for £20 for Eccleston, a good man. In comparison to those of the present day the fee is ridiculously small, but still it came in very useful, and was much appreciated by that unfortunate official who enjoyed the doubtful honour of presiding over the financial department.

During the whole of the Summer and part of the ensuing Winter a capital joke was the order of the day. It arose quite in a simple way. A typical Scotchman, McKenzie by name, was manager for Calder's Creosote Works on the Alexandra Dock and a few of us were seated in the White Hart, when the name of the Celtic Football Club was mentioned. For a joke I stated that the Celts really ought to be called Kelts, in fact they were not Scotch at all. McKenzie, as I expected, at once took it up. The conversation got warm, but I offered to prove my assertion. On reaching home, having learned a little of Latin and Greek in the old days at Lord Browne's School, I hunted up the old dictionary and found that the Latin word Celt was derived from the

Greek word Keatos, and that this was the name of a primitive race that existed in the South of Europe, and were the inhabitants of caverns. Armed with this information I got a friend to write a letter I dictated to him to be sent to Dundee, and then posted to me. In the meantime McKenzie had written to no less a person than Professor Blackie. When we next met with the usual crowd, man says, "Now you (Capital B—— Mr. Printer), I have got you. Here's a letter from Professor Blackie," which of course stated Celtic was the proper pronunciation. Just in the hour of his triumph, as he imagined, I pulled mine out. It was to the effect that the Kelts were originally the primitive inhabitants of caverns in the South of Europe, but wandered through Ireland, until they eventually settled in the North of Scotland. This letter was signed " Peter McWhitey." Imagine Mac's rage. "What you (Capital B again, Mr. Printer), I come from Ireland, etc." But I carried the crowd with me, as I argued that my informant at all events had a Mac in front of his name, whereas Professor Blackie had not.

Being in the know I found out that McKenzie had sent a letter to Professor McWhitey's address in Dundee, and accordingly got fully armed to meet the charge. When we next met I could see the gleam of triumph glitter in Mac's eye, and he accosted me thus: "Come here (I won't trouble you to produce the Capital B's this time, Mr. Printer, you would require quite a case) I wrote to Professor McWhitey at Dundee, and here's the envelope countersigned fourteen times 'address not known.' What do you think to that?" said Mac, indulging in the sanguinary once more. I simply said "I am not surprised, as I have received a letter from him from Skegness, where is having a holiday," and I at once produced it. Eventually, alter a tremendous amount of fun, which it caused in not a few cocoa houses shall I say, Mac settled the affair by standing a bottle of the best Scotch, and we were afterwards the best of friends. It is consoling to know that although Mac was chaffed unmercifully for quite a number of weeks through the argument, he became the possessor of an autograph letter from Professor Blackie, which he treasures to this day.

With the near approach of the season a large number of supporters were of opinion that sufficient new blood had not been obtained for the ensuing arduous season, but it was quite an erroneous idea, for the quintette that had already arrived in the Fisheries were distinctly above the average, as their performances in the League amply proved ere the season terminated.

Unfortunately when the Cup Ties came round we once more experienced the cruel luck of having to work our way through the Qualifying Round. The first three matches, Staveley, Kilnhurst, and Lincoln City, all were away from home. Having dealt with them, Rotherham were beaten at Abbey Park, which landed us in the Competition once more. In the first Round our bad luck still continued, and after we had surprised not a few by beating Darwin away from home we did have a ray of sunshine inasmuch as we were drawn at home against the celebrated West Bromwich Albion. Naturally great preparations were made for a record crowd. Charges for admission were raised as follows 6d. and 1s., 1s. extra for covered stands, and 3s. 6d. for reserved seats, numbered, on covered stand. When the day arrived, every available seat was occupied, a record gate assembled, and after a desperate struggle it terminated in a drawn game. The following Wednesday, however, when we visited the Brum district, they were too good for us, thanks to the brilliant form shown by Billy Bassett, then at his best, and the Cup Ties for that season were once more of no interest to Grimsby Town.

Naturally the finances received a very welcome addition, and possibly if the bazaar had been the success anticipated the Team might have been retained another season, but unfortunately, despite the great efforts made by the chairman, F. B. Coulson, and his Committee, the amount handed over by the Chairman was only some £270, which caused the Directors to accept the offer of Aston Villa for Whitehouse's transfer. Of course the Directorate came in for an awful slating from the usual crowd, but, candidly speaking, they had no alternative. The reason was not far to seek. For years the bird had been bad, indeed just now it was in a state of collapse, and it was with a sigh of relief that all concerned saw the last of that blessed bird.

If for nothing else the season was noticeable for a record achieved by the Town in the home matches that stood quite alone throughout the country, namely, they were unbeaten at home. In fact, up to the very last match, against Woolwich Arsenal, which resulted in a draw, they had won every match, a grand performance when the calibre of their opponents is considered. As usual they finished well up, just outside the test matches, and the record will bear inspection :—

Matches				Goals		
Played	Won	Drawn	Lost	For	Against	Points
30	19	8	3	76	38	41

If ever a club appeared to have the test matches within their grasp, Grimsby Town had this season, for they only had to beat Walsall at home to make it certain. I well remember the day when the latter arrived. Several of us met them at the station, and having adjourned to Ye White Harte for a wee drappie, the conversation naturally turned on the match. The visitors, in a jocular sort of manner saying, "If you win today you are safe for the test matches, and as we are very comfortable here, you might as well leave a quid for a drink or two." Personally I don't think for a moment they seriously thought of it, but all the same, when they won, after having all the worst of the game, by about the biggest fluke on record, it struck some of us that if the opportunity had occurred in Lancashire a little whiskey would have been the order of the day. It is no exaggeration to say that losing this match made a difference of at least £500 to Grimsby Town.

This journey the annual meeting was quite a treat. An optimistic feeling prevailed that at length Grimsby Town were on a fairly sound footing, financially and otherwise, and therefore little criticism was offered to the Directors' record for the past season. Although not mentioned the financial position of every team of note had been materially improved by the passage of the rule by the League re transfer fees. Take Whitehouse's case for instance. Clearly through this Grimsby Town had raised sufficient of the all necessary to at length clear themselves of the old debts and had they not on their books new players of more than average value. Therefore to all appearances the optimistic feeling was quite justified.

When the meeting of the League was held, W. H. Bellamy was once more elected on the Committee, a very satisfactory item so far as we were concerned, and we likewise had a stroke of luck when Gainsborough Trinity were elected to the Second Division, which gave us an attractive fixture destined to last for many years.

As usual quite a batch of new players arrived, two goalkeepers, Cain and Wallace, Chapman and Morris, Welsh Internationals; Hogan, J. Rodgers and Munn. Cain was an awful frost. Wallace, brilliant occasionally, was destined to wreck Grimsby Town's prospects in the future. Hogan, Munn and Chapman nothing out of the ordinary, leaving Morris and J. Rodgers as class men.

It is satisfactory to note that for the first time on record Grimsby Town were exempted from the qualifying rounds of the English Cup, and in the competition proper had the luck to be drawn against Bolton Wanderers at Abbey Park. Although a matter of sixteen years since, it can safely be said, not even including the Bradford City match, has there been an English Cup Tie cause so much excitement in this district. Preparations were made for a tremendous crowd, excursions were run by the various Railway Companies, and such was the demand for tickets that the prices were advanced for the best stands. Here they are :— Admission 6d. and 1s., special stands 1s. extra, Hazelgrove stand 2s. extra, reserved portion, carpeted and numbered 4s., including admission to ground. When the day arrived the ground was speedily packed, and after a grand exposition of the game, especially by the goalkeepers, Sutcliffe and Wallace, it resulted in a tie. By-the-bye, Sutcliffe, who figured between the sticks, was originally a Rugby international player in the Heckmondwike team. He was a tremendous punter, and through this alone he was persuaded to join the trotters and embrace the Soccer code. How he eventually played international for England is a matter of history. By doing this he was the first man in England to have an International Cap for both codes.

After the tie the excitement increased and arrangements were made for the excursion to Bolton, but King Frost intervened, and the match was postponed. When it came off Sutcliffe, through a certain reason, was not between the sticks, but they had a very efficient substitute, and once more a tie was the result. Ordered to play off on neutral ground, Bramall Lane, Sheffield, was selected. Excursions were run from all parts, and Bolton Wanderers, fearing the Town, were once more determined to have Sutcliffe in the team, but it was a near thing. By some means or other his trial took place that very morning for an assault. He was fined, which was, of course, paid, and he went straight to the station, and just landed on the field in time. It was easily seen the sympathies of the crowd were with us, and when we led at half-time apparently it was a good thing for the Town. Early in the second half our front line was all over the Trotter's defence, and never before or since have I seen three such fine corners as were put in by Joe Rodgers in succession. With anyone in goal but Sutcliffe we must have scored but he cleared splendidly. Even then we looked like winning, but to the surprise and disgust of every follower of the Town Wallace allowed two of the softest goals I have ever seen to be scored, and we were defeated. The general opinion was that Wallace had been squared, but personally I think it was an attack of nerves, and also occasionally, I am convinced, Wallace, was not responsible for his actions.

Throughout the whole of this season Fletcher and McCairns had been showing magnificent form, and when the period arrived for the selection of the team for the trial matches prior to the International one, Fletcher was amongst the selected. Last season he was within an ace of being capped, and we all thought at length his merits were going to be recognised. McCairns actually was also selected at the last moment, but unfortunately there was no train available to land him in time. Hard lines for Tommy.

After a lapse of several years it was quite a novelty to be engaged in the Lincoinshire Cup once more. It cannot, however, be said that there was anything like the excitement knocking about that there was in the old days. Of course, once more we won it, defeating the Cits. easily enough in the final by six goals to two, a victory never in doubt, as. this season at all events, we were streets in front of anything in the Fen County. For several seasons we had always finished on the verge of the test matches, and this season was no exception to the rule, as we finished third. Hard lines, indeed, as not only did it mean a loss of quite £200 financially, but on form we had more than an outside chance of fighting our way through the test matches into the first League. This record will bear inspection.

Matches				Goals		
Played	Won	Drawn	Lost	For	Against	Points
30	17	9	4	71	46	38

It is somewhat singular that taking it all round the strength of our opponents in the other matches was not so good. We did not have quite such a good average. Here it is

Matches				Goals		
Played	Won	Drawn	Lost	For	Against	Points
52	29	14	9	139	90	

When the annual meeting was held it was very evident that nothing like the optimistic tone of the previous year prevailed. In fact the keynote was struck quite differently when the financial statement was made. True, we had cleared the Hazelgrove stand, and made alterations on the ground, but still it was very evident, or at least should have been to those present, that Grimsby Town was on the very fringe of a financial crisis, and clearly they were wise in carrying the motion of the Chairman that the offer should be accepted of certain gentlemen taking bonds for £600, with the ground appointments of the Club as security. I must acknowledge myself that the said gentlemen evidently had the interests of the Club at heart, for to say the least the security was exceedingly doubtful, simply because the lease of the ground was rapidly nearing its termination with no chance of its being renewed.

As per usual a large number of new arrivals were announced, Whittaker, goal, McLean, Richardson, Gouldie, Harrison, Mount and Hyde, and a precious sample they were. In fact, Whittaker and Gouldie were the only pair at all worthy of donning the colours of Grimsby Town. Later George Mountain (Bodge) joined as a forward. In comparison to some of the others his services were priceless, simply because at all events he had the common honesty of always being a trier.

This season it had been decided to give McCairns and Harry Fletcher a benefit, and they both duly came off. Considering the bad form shown by the team generally, and naturally the public having a number nine hump, both of them had reason to be satisfied with the amount of the all necessary handed over to them, but all the same it was exceedingly hard lines, for Harry Fletcher especially, after his grand services to the Club, that his benefit should have been fixed for this season. How to account for the wretched form shown by the Team throughout the season is more or less a problem, but still no doubt to a great extent it was firstly through the lack of firmness shown by the Directors in dealing with a certain section of the players, and secondly the absurd idea of a number of skippers, who, apparently thinking any football player was a little god, made enormous sacrifices to be in his company, which, of course, invariably ended in the said player being "canned up."

After the brilliant form shown last year in the memorable matches with Bolton Wanderers, it was thought that at least in the English Competition some form would be shown, but instead of this, when Notts. Forest were met at Nottingham they gave about the worst exposition of the game it has ever been my lot to witness. True the Foresters eventually won the Cup, but I venture to make the assertion that if it had been the Town team of the preceding year a very different result would have been chronicled.

With the Cup Ties a thing of the past the majority of the supporters were exceedingly glad when April arrived and we were on the eve of ringing the curtain down. It is an old saying, "Comparisons are odious," and this season it was very applicable to their doings. As far as the League was concerned the record, just by way of a change, won't bear inspection. Here it is :—

Matches				Goals		
Played	Won	Drawn	Lost	For	Against	Points
30	10	 16	 4	 52	62	 24

For the first time it will be noticed that the goal average was against us, a novelty, indeed, so far as the Grimsby Town Club was concerned. Fortunately, badly as they played there were one or two very weak clubs in the competition this season, which alone kept us from the indignity of having to apply for admission by virtue of finishing in the last three. Perhaps the two most noticeable items of this disastrous season were firstly that Harry Fletcher, after his benefit, was transferred to Notts. County — the latter were just then in a desperate position, in fact fighting for their very existence in the First Division, but after the arrival of Harry Fletcher they never looked back; in fact it is no exaggeration at all to say that to him at once have Notts. County to thank that they retained their position in the First League — the second was that Mr. Frank Hazelgrove, having resigned his position as financial secretary, Harry Hickson, who had been clerk to the Club since August 10th, 1896, was appointed secretary, which appointment he has held ever since, a period of sixteen years.

It was very creditable to all concerned that it was decided after the disastrous season, in common parlance, to take the bull by the horns and amongst other ideas mooted was that of a working men's committee. A meeting was duly held, Oliver Best in the chair, at which a brother scribe, Mr. A. Martin, of the Telegraph, announced that one had been formed at Lincoln which was a great success. Perhaps it was, by some means or other, but although a certain amount of revenue was received through this Committee, it failed to take on quite as well as expected, much to the regret of the pioneers of the movement.

1898-9.

Re the team, it was clearly apparent the Directorate were tired of the old crowd, and literally a clean sweep was made, only Bodge Mountain and Bell being retained. The new men, it is satisfactory to note, had only one Scotchman amongst them, but perhaps such a novelty as a brand new team is worth giving in full. Here it is.

Bagshaw, Gainsborough Trinity.
Steward, Newcastle United.
Pennington, Bristol East Ville Rovers.
S. C. Herry, Hamilton Academicals.
P. Gray, Liverpool.
J. Griffiths, Aston Villa.
W. Greenwood, Warmley.
H. Chapman, Rochdale.
J. W. Cockshot, Reading.
G. Radcliffe, Stone Town.
B. Jenkinson, Sheffield United.
A. Nelmes, Middlesbrough.
C. Richards.
Nidd.

It will be noticed that amongst the above were three of the most popular professionals who ever arrived in Grimsby, each of whom did great service for the Town, I allude to Paddy Gray, C. Richards and Happy Nelmes. Whilst on the subject of the new players just a line for one of the old, namely Harry Fletcher. For several seasons I have remarked he deserved certain honours, and this year at length his abilities were recognised, and if he did not get his International Cap he got the League one, in the opinion of not a few of far greater merit than the more coveted cap bestowed on all Internationals.

At the meeting of the League to the satisfaction of the football world it was decided to abolish the Test Matches and instead admit to the Upper House in an automatic way by the two top clubs in the Second Division moving up and the two bottom clubs having the Irishman's lift into the Second Division. This caused the League to be increased to forty clubs, and so it remains to this day. Various attempts have been made to alter it, but up to date their efforts have been futile.

In the English Cup once more we were destined to reach the Competition proper. Mexborough, Lincoln City at home, and Barnsley away, were easy victim, but we dropped across a rough fence when we were drawn away to play Preston North End. I don't suppose for a moment the most rabid supporter of Grimsby Town expected us to win, but still a rout of seven clear goals was very warm. Various excuses were made, but to sum it up briefly just for once the Directorate were caught napping, and the men were not properly shod considering the sea of mud they had to play upon.

In the Lincolnshire Competition quite a different class of clubs were met, and just by way of a change Gainsborough Trinity obliged the Cits, by relieving them of any further interest in the Competition, only to have the same operation performed upon them in the final by Grimsby Town. Unfortunately, however, little interest was taken in the Competition, thanks to the League fixtures.

This season, by no stretch of the imagination could the form shown in the League be satisfactory in comparison to the large outlay on new players. True we finished sixth, in the top half of the table, but something far different to this was expected when the season commenced, and naturally all concerned were disappointed when the table was finally cast up. As usual the finances were rather rocky, and once more those willing to work had to put their shoulders to the wheel, promoting a grand concert and ball at the Town Hall and an archery tournament. Both were a success, and the exchequer received a much needed fillip.

1899-1900.

With no possibility of renewing the lease the Directorate, of course, were experiencing a large amount of anxiety re securing a ground. Mr. Alcock, however, came to the rescue, and offered Blundell Park. Negotiations ensued, and eventually everything was arranged satisfactorily, and the Grimsby Town flag was once more unfurled on the Cleethorpes Road. It scarcely requires a Solomon to know that this was the correct pitch for a football ground, but all the same I think the Directorate made a tremendous mistake in leasing the ground from Mr. Alcock. Let it be understood, I do not blame the latter

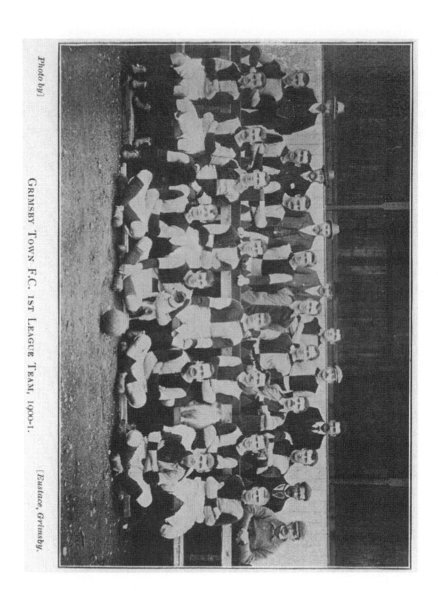

Photo by]

GRIMSBY TOWN F.C. 1ST LEAGUE TEAM, 1900-1.

(Eustace, Grimsby.

in the slightest. Indeed he is to be commended for a smart business transaction in securing Grimsby Town as tenants, but I do blame the Directorate at that time in command of Grimsby Town for not making an attempt to secure a ground of their own. True, their financial position was not sound, and I may say without fear of contradiction that I have had a thorough grounding in football finance, and know exactly what that means, but, instead of this preventing them from making the attempt, in my opinion it should have had a contra effect. Let us look at it from my point of view. It is simply my old idea advanced re Clee Park. Purchase the freehold and form a proper athletic club. To have done this, a piece of land, say seven or eight acres, should have been bought, and I have reason to believe it could have been obtained then quite adjacent to Blundell Park on the same side of the road for say £4,000. This with the laying out, would have meant, say £6,000, and you would have had a permanent home, Capitalised at five per cent., this was only a matter of £300 a year, or six pounds a week. A large amount, did I hear someone say? Not at all. Why, almost half could easily have been had for advertising alone, but this is not the only thing in its favour. Do not let us lose sight of the fact that during the struggle from a financial point of view every Football Club is bound to have through Summer wages, etc. The value of that land on Cleethorpe Road would. have been increasing by leaps and bounds, and naturally the Directorate would have been armed with an asset the value of which can scarcely be estimated. If any further proof were wanted that this is the correct policy, how is it that Everton, Newcastle, Sheffield United, etc., in fact the majority of the richest clubs, have purchased their freehold? Why, even Hull City, which is presided over by a financial expert, attempted to do the same this season. Surely the answer is simple. In fact it is already answered up aloft, but it may be as well to note that there is such a thing as a Football Club collapsing. If this did occur would not this land be ripe for building purposes. It is the right pitch, and if it was worth £4,000 in 1900 it is worth at least £6,000 now.

Even now the Directors are playing with fire, to use a metaphor, unless they have secured a long lease, as absolutely the only pitch, viz., in Grimsby Road, is rapidly becoming built on. I have digressed somewhat on the subject, but all the same it would be a wise policy for them to secure a plot of land ere it is too late in this district, the splendid tram services alone being an important factor.

Naturally it was unreasonable to expect on the opening of the season that the ground would be in perfect order, and as per usual the grumblers had quite a happy time, but still signs were not wanting that in the immediate future Grimsby Town would possess a ground immeasurably superior to anything they had previously had. In fact it was rapidly being completed in a manner suitable for First League Football.

With Whitehouse returning to the fold it was thought that we even now had an outside chance of topping the League, but instead were destined to have rather a poor season. In fact, although we finished in the upper half of the table it was in a great measure attributable to the fact that all round the clubs comprising the Second Division were scarcely as strong as in the preceding year. Neither did we do anything great in the Cup Competition, and it was with a sigh of relief that the curtain was rung down on this season.

1900-1901.

Notwithstanding the moderate success of the preceding season an optimistic tone prevailed throughout the Town amongst the Directors and supporters that at last a determined effort should be made to enter the First Division of the League. With this object in view no expense was spared in getting the best available talent, and ere the season commenced the following players were available :— Harris, Mountain, Leiper (captain), Griffiths, Gray, Nelmes, Jenkinson, Hall, Walker, Richards, Leigh, Mellor, Hemingfield, McEvoy, Lakey, and later on with Fletcher returning from Notts. County and McFarlane arriving, it was very evident we were determined to have a powerful team to make the attempt.

This season we did not shine in the Cup Competition, neither did we want particularly, so it was indeed a blessing in disguise when we got knocked out and thus were in a position to concentrate our efforts on the attempt to capture the flag. If this were accomplished the Team were offered a very substantial bonus, likewise if they finished second, and early on it was very apparent business was meant. Throughout the season the utmost excitement prevailed, and when the Town by drawing at Middlesbrough reached the goal they had been striving for the enthusiasm was intense. For reference I append the names of the Team that took the field at Middlesbrough.

Goal, McFarlane.

Backs, G. Mountain and J. Leiper.

Half-backs, Hemingfield, Gray and Nelmes.

Forwards, Fletcher, Hall, Leigh, Mellor and Watkins.

Afterwards a dinner was held at the Oberon, plenty of toys, &c., including a wee drappie, to celebrate the occasion. Great enthusiasm was shown when the Team stepped up to receive their share of the bonus, £200, which was divided equally, and who will deny that they deserved it.

The Directorate were so delighted at reaching the height of their ambition that they decided to have medals to celebrate the event, and very handsome ones they were too, costing about a fiver each, and being about the size of that Yankee gold piece the 20 dollar. On the front in the centre there was the coat of arms of the Borough, the three boar heads, and round the rim "League Championship 2nd Division 1900-1," with the flags entwined. The reverse side "H. Hickson, Secretary," in the centre, and round the rim "Winners of Lincolnshire Cup 1900-1, Grimsby Town Football Club."

Not content with this triumph the Team thought it necessary to once more win the Lincolnshire Cup. Rather an insignificant bauble in comparison to the great achievement noted above, but considering it carried some gold medals with it perhaps that induced the Team to make the effort. Just once more our friends the Cits. were the victims, and really it is nothing short of remarkable that they seemed utterly unable to extend Grimsby Town in Cup Ties.

At the general meeting a fairly satisfactory balance sheet was shown, roughly as follows.

	£	s.	d.
Receipts	4,360	16	5
Expenses	4,185	18	9
Balance in hand	174	17	8

Last year the receipts were £2,061 18s. 2d. A casual glance is quite sufficient to prove this season the receipts had been doubled, in fact we were getting at last amongst the so-called wealthy clubs, but alas one little item had been overlooked by not a few, namely that this season no less than £1,287 4s. 10d. had been received by the archery tournament and transfer fees. Of course, bar possibly a few transfer fees, this was scarcely likely to reappear for some years to come, and with the Summer wages to find and the responsibility of practically having to secure a new team strong enough to carry us in the upper house, the Directorate were faced with a gigantic task. It is quite common for the average supporter of a club to imagine that if a team is good enough to win a position in the upper house it is good enough to maintain it. Nothing can be more absurd than this idea, as it has been proved many a time. Evidently the Directorate thought so too, for they made an onslaught directly the clock struck twelve on the 1st May and signed on no less than five men of the Queen's Park Rangers, namely Ronaldson, Bellingham, Skinner, Clutterbuck and McConnell. In addition to these Dean, of Notts., A. Gardner, Harper, and Whittaker, were secured, so with the best of the old team available, bar MacFarlane, who returned to the Celtic, apparently a team had been secured quite capable of holding its own in the First League.

It may be as well to note that this season a local, hailing from Meg's Island, rapidly came to the front and opened the eyes of not a few of the Directors that came with our First Division guests and early on it was very evident that Grimsby Town had secured a magnet in the football world. I allude to Appleyard. How he eventually was snapped up by Newcastle United and was destined to narrowly miss getting his cap can easily be remembered by the present generation. Yes, he was a good man, perhaps not quite tricky enough for Newcastle, but he took some stopping, and for several seasons was the deadliest shot in England.

SEASON 1901-2.

With the stands resplendent in a new coat of paint the championship flag of the Second Division gaily flying in the, breeze, and the ground literally packed, Derby County appeared as our first visitors to open the First League campaign. They brought a powerful team including Bloomer, then in his prime, but the Town quite held their own, in fact were unlucky not to win, the tie, one each, scarcely being a true record of the play. The following team represented the Town :—

Goal, Tennant.

Backs, Mountain and Leiper.

Half-Backs, Hemingfield, Bellingham and Nelmes.

Forwards, Dean, Harper, Ronaldson, Leigh and Gardner.

Considerable anxiety was felt by the Directors whether the attendance of the public would be large enough to enable them to run really a first-class team, and it is satisfactory to note that £234 was taken at the gates. Of course in comparison with several of the clubs I could mention it appeared absurdly small, but still when everything is considered this was thought satisfactory, and with a little luck in the Cup Ties the Directorate were confident that sufficient of the all necessary would be gathered in to meet expenses for the current season.

Unfortunately the Team, through various causes, struck a bad pitch, not through bad play altogether, but there was more than a suspicion we were not treated fairly by some of the officials appointed for our fixtures. Generally speaking I always have been dead against attributing improper motives to those behind the whistle, but on several occasions decisions were given against the Town, which meant losing points, that were to say the least peculiar. Whatever the cause was is immaterial, but when half-time arrived in the new year the record for Grimsby Town was anything but lively. Here it is :—

Matches				Goals		
Played	Won	Drawn	Lost	For	Against	Points
17	4	2	11	14	36	10

Afterwards with Whittaker in goal the form shown was much better, in fact during March we seemed quite safe, but after the way we were defeated at Stoke on April 14th, it was evident that there was something behind the scenes. Yes, we were not wanted in the Upper House. By fair means or foul a coalition had been formed to "out" us. Our position became precarious, but eventually in the very last match, at Liverpool, our team made their position secure for another season by making a tie of it, much to the satisfaction of all lovers of the game in the Fisheries. If any proof was required that the teams were just about of equal merit it will be noticed that although Grimsby Town averaged nearly a point per match, they only just did the trick. Here is the record :—

Matches				Goals		
Played	Won	Drawn	Lost	For	Against	Points
34	13	6	15	46	57	32

Naturally the simple wire announcing that the momentous fixture with Liverpool had resulted in a draw of 2 goals each, thus enabling the Town to retain its position in the First League, caused any amount of enthusiasm in the Fisheries. Immediately the wire arrived some of the Nuts, notably Fred Beels and. Bob Chapman, who were engaged in the agreeable occupation of cocking their nebs into something both soothing and refreshing at Hodges, decided to celebrate the occasion, and messengers were at once despatched to summon a band to meet the team on their arrival home early in the morning. The following artistes duly appeared:—

E. Killoran, senr. (euphonium), Bob Peel (tenor horn), Harry Kent, the well-known butcher (flute), Jack Scott (cornet), Freddy Beels (big drum). On arriving at the Town Station at least 1,000 enthusiastic followers were present. The enthusiasm was intense. On the train arriving, the "Conquering Hero" was at once struck up. Yes, things in general were very lively. Trams were taken as far as the Docks Station, where all got out, the band duly formed in line, with Alf. Martin, an old friend of mine in the journalistic world, as Drum-Major, with the Directors, Chris. White, W. H. Bellamy, &c., and about 1,000 others marched in procession to the Lincoln Arms. Mr. W. H. Bellamy, in a few well chosen words, thanked Mr. Beels, the remainder of the Band, and supporters, for the grand reception they had given the team, and thus ended one of the most memorable days in the annals of Grimsby Town.

This season Bodge was entitled to a benefit, but unfortunately for him the Cits. were the bill of fare. Truth to tell the general public were just sick of having this team rung upon them for this purpose, and the result was that although Bodge got a fair benefit the amount was of nothing like the dimensions it should have been. Perhaps it would have been larger if he had come from across the Border instead of being a local.

This season our career so far as the English Cup Ties were concerned was very satisfactory. True we got beaten in the First Round, but only in the second attempt, Portsmouth tieing with us at Blundell Park, one each, and beating us in the replay by two to none. Possibly the most satisfactory part, of it was the exchequer received a much needed lift, and the, financial secretary assumed a double-six smile that had ,not appeared once since the season commenced. The receipts were as follows :—

	£
At Grimsby	374
At Portsmouth	576
Total	950

a very nice egg. It is possibly worth noting that this is the team that introduced the well-known cry of "Helloe." How it did ring in your ears to be sure. Naturally our crowd took it up and astonished not a few of our opponents when they accompanied our team to Bramall Lane and other grounds.

At the termination of the season Mr. Alcock generously decided to give a dinner to the team, officials and friends, at the Imperial Hotel. With a record attendance, everything of the best provided, the toast list limited, and a fair sprinkling of vocalists, just for once life was worth living, at least that was the opinion formed by yours truly.

1902-3.

Notwithstanding the remarkable increase of revenue the finances were in anything but a prosperous condition but the policy of the Directorate remained unchanged. They were determined to have yet a better team if possible and Dunn Atherton, and Dave Gardner, from Newcastle United, were safely landed. These, with Long, Glen, Spendiff, Williams, Paterson and Singleton, to all appearances brought the Team up to concert pitch, and looked on paper quite strong enough to hold its' own.

When our prospects seemed of the brightest a veritable bombshell, as it were, exploded in our midst, for the English Association at their meeting had the cool effrontery to suspend the whole of our Team that played at Stoke on April 14th for one week. Luckily for us Notts. Forest proved true friends and kindly consented to alter the date of their match with us to September 9th. True by doing so our gate may have been affected somewhat, as it was played on the Tuesday night, but still it was a kindness much appreciated in this quarter of the globe, and showed conclusively how deep our friendship still was with the merrie Foresters.

After the match a variety of opinions were expressed as to the merits of our team, the majority thinking we should figure high up in the list. Personally I did not think so, and the result was my opinion was ridiculed and after a good deal of chaff, although never a betting man, I had a few new hats on, which, needless to say, I won.

As the season advanced it was very evident that it would only be by a desperate effort we should retain our position in the League, but certainly it is nothing short of remarkable that when half time arrived in the new year our record of points should be precisely the same as the preceding year, as follows

Matches				Goals		
Played	Won	Drawn	Lost	For	Against	Points
18	2	6	10	24	38	10

In the new year the Team was sent to Matlock to train, and the first ray of sunshine was seen during the season. I allude to the victory over.Aston Villa, at Birmingham. This was the first victory away, and it was thought that at last the tide had turned, but alas they were doomed to disappointment as subsequent events proved.

Once more the period for the First Round of the English Cup was near at hand, and this journey we could not complain of our luck, as we had Newcastle United for our bill of fare. Elaborate preparations were made on the grounds and a new scale of admission was charged as follows :—

Cleethorpes Road End, 6d.

Harrington Street, 1s.

Uncovered portion of stand A and B, 1s. 6d. with admission.

Covered portion, 2s.

Centre portion reserved, 2s. 6d.

Stand transfers, 6d. extra.

Naturally a good crowd assembled and the match proved very exciting. Appleyard in particular showed fine form. At half time the Town led two to none, but Newcastle scored twenty minutes before time, and there was just a chance of a draw, but the Town defended well and eventually won by two to one. It is satisfactory to note that although the gate was nothing like so much as expected, £337 was taken, leaving a fair balance to the Town after all demands had been met.

Once more we were favoured in the draw, Notts. County being our visitors. According to form there looked like being one more victory, and we seemed destined to finish in the last eight of the Competition, but to our surprise the

Lambs proved rather easy victors by two goals to nil. Perhaps they were lucky. As a matter of fact they were, as on the run of the game we should at least have drawn, but after all it is goals that count, and therefore they must be given credit for a smart performance. The gate was a record for Grimsby Town, £496 being taken. Perhaps it will be interesting to compare the gates in the competition this year with the last.

	£
At Grimsby	374
At Portsmouth	576
Total	950
Newcastle United at Grimsby	337
Notts. County at Grimsby	495
Total	832

a difference of £118 against us.

With all the interest in the Cup a thing of the past it was centred in the League Competition. A determined effort was made to steer clear of the last two. For a time our prospects were bright, but signs were not wanting that undue pressure and influence were working secretly against us. Up to the very last match we had a chance. If we had beaten Aston Villa at the Park and Blackburn Rovers had lost at Newcastle, we should have beaten them on goal average, but it was not to be, as we lost against the Villa and finished in the seventeenth position, Bolton Wanderers being at the bottom. Our record was as follows :—

Matches				Goals		
Played	Won	Drawn	Lost	For	Against	Points
34	8	17	9	43	63	25

The test matches of bygone years had been more or less a scandal, but this season it was apparent to the veriest novice that Blackburn Rovers had been deliberately given four points by Bury and Everton, two Lancashire teams. Just now both of them were in grand form, and yet the Rovers won both of these matches away from home. The Everton match was so glaring that their own press announced that the Everton team were hissed and hooted by their own spectators, a proof at least of the old adage that Englishmen like fair play. The pace became so hot that Mr. W. H. Bellamy, one of the most fearless advocates that ever represented the Club, caused a meeting to be held and accused the Secretary of the Blackburn Rovers, a Mr. Waumsley, of attempting to bribe both the Bury and Everton players. Evidently there was something in it, for it resulted in Mr. Waumsley being suspended for life from participating in football management. Unfortunately although the various Directorates concerned were guilty enough the charge could not be fully proved, and they escaped. Of course, if they had been convicted we should have gained our position in the First Division, as no doubt Everton, Bury and the Rovers would have had to retire from the League or else be suspended for a long period, which would have been an equivalent to the same.

Possibly the one ray of sunshine during the season was the winning of the Lincolnshire Cup. Compared to bygone days the interest now was practically nil, but still it filled a vacant date, and we once more beat the Cits.

Naturally as the season advanced the finances became in a dangerous condition, and an appeal was made to the supporters, etc., of the club to pay an additional sixpence for admission to the remaining three League matches to be played at the Park, namely Liverpool, West Bromwich Albion and Aston Villa. Unfortunately this had a contra effect on the attendance, in fact the gates were less than usual, not very consoling to the Directorate considering they were faced with a deficit of about £1,510 besides that little item of summer wages. Lively for the Directors wasn't it? Talk about the old bird buried years ago, what about this? It must have been big enough for an elephant. Naturally there was only one alternative, realising on their players. As usual the leading clubs were keen enough, tempting offers were made, and the following players migrated :—

Appleyard, Newcastle United.
Ronaldson, Bury.
Hall, Derby County.
Whittaker, Derby County.
Glen, Notts. County.
Mountain, Leicester Fosse.

1903-4.

Considerable interest was taken in the general meeting, and tall figures were knocking about. Here are a few :—

Gate receipts, £4,606 18s.
Transfer fees, £1,260.
Total receipts, £6,183 9s. 2d.
Players' wages, £3,131 0s. 10d.
Paid for players, £500 10s.
Balance due to bank, £137 5s.

Here's a lively lot of figures to juggle with. That freehold ground would have been a real asset now, would it not?

Practically the old Directorate were elected, Fred Coulson as chairman, W. H. Bellamy financial secretary, but to the dismay of all Chris White definitely decided to resign his position as chairman of the Management Committee. This was a serious loss to the Club, as he had put in a tremendous amount of work, simply for the love of the game. Although never a pessimist I think the majority of the people will agree with me that the last two seasons proved conclusively that it was practically an impossibility for First Division football to pay in Grimsby. Here we had an income of over £6,000 for one season, a supposed good team, and yet events proved they could not win sufficient matches to occupy a good position in the League, which alone draws good gates. We also had exceptional luck in the English Cup Competition both years. No, it is useless denying we are so terribly handicapped by our geographical position, lack of population, etc., that I for one even in this present year, when I am inflicting this on you, am of opinion that it is infinitely better in the true interests of Grimsby Town to be winning matches in the Second Division than to be struggling at the bottom of the First. Of course, I know the well-known cry of a certain section "We must be in the First at all costs." Yes, quite so, but invariably they are the very first to keep away if the team are down on their luck, and the Directorate can go to — well, not Cleethorpes. I have had some.

Later on this season the Fish Merchants played the Fish Salesmen a football match at Blundell Park for the benefit of the Charities, the Merchants winning by two goals to one. I don't know whether Will C., who organised the match, got the odd goal scored by the Salesmen, but I do know he captured a duck in the cricket match. How was your appetite, Bill? It is very satisfactory to note that in the two matches, cricket and football, sufficient of the all necessary was taken to hand over the following to those deserving charities.

	£	s
Hull Orphan Home	26	5
Grimsby Nursing Home	10	10

It says much for the pluck of the Directorate that the following players were engaged for the attempt to regain the First Division :— A. McConnell, C. Roberts, J. McDiarmid, J. Nichols, J. Miller, W. Wilkinson, and J. McAllister. It scarcely requires a Solomon to select the pick of this catch. Yes, there was one pearl, Charlie Roberts, the remainder, with the exception of McConnell, being nothing out of the ordinary. The result easily proved this, as, for the first half of the season the form shown was wretched in the extreme, and when half-time arrived they were only tenth on the table, with the following record :—

Matches				Goals		
Played	Won	Drawn	Lost	For	Against	Points
14	5	4	5	18	21	14

During the Christmas holidays better form was shown. Barnsley and Edinburgh St. Bernard's being beaten by five to one. By-the-bye, the latter team is the one McBeth and Riddock came from when they crossed the Border. To those in the know it was not at all surprising that owing to the bad form shown by the team friction should arise amongst the shareholders and supporters of the Club, but it was ever thus. A victim, or rather victims, had to be found, and this journey a certain section endeavoured to put the blame upon the Chairman and Financial Secretary. Fortunately both of them were level-headed, treated this with contempt, and decided to lay low until the season terminated. It is satisfactory to note that after all the Team did not hold half a bad position in the League, with the following record :—

Matches				Goals		
Played	Won	Drawn	Lost	For	Against	Points
34	14	8	12	50	49	36

1904-5.

Whether the malcontents saw the red light is more or less a problem, but when a special meeting of shareholders was held at the King's Hall on May 6th sulphur was in the air. For a start the officials who had the distinguished honour — I don't think — of having the onus of attempting to wreck the Club during the preceding season, thrown at them, threatened to resign, but strange to say there was an unanimous opinion that they should continue at the helm, but they were on their dignity. Even a worm will turn, and they absolutely declined to continue in office without some scheme was formulated which would put the Club on a sound basis from a financial point of view. Various suggestions were made, such as the remaining shares being taken up, about a thousand, but like many other ideas it was not practicable, besides one clause affecting them, namely, that a shareholder having one share should be entitled to a seat on the Directorate, was prejudicial to the true interests of the Club, for a very simple reason. It is more than probable that he might not be in a position to sign a guarantee at the bank, a most necessary Operation, as, without this, it is utterly impossible to hand that small slip over the mahogany which is the "open sesame" for the all necessary required to work the team. It is satisfactory to note that as a preliminary to the general meeting a vote of thanks was passed to all the directors, etc., for their services during the past season.

The general meeting held at the Oberon Hotel on May 25th was practical in every respect. F. B. Coulson was in the chair, the usual forest of figures was shot out to juggle with. I should imagine a great proportion of those present looked upon these something like we youngsters in our school days did on the fifth problem of euclid, "Pons Asinorum" (the ass's bridge), which floored Tichborne in his trial, as something beyond their conception. However, it scarcely required a Solomon to note although on paper we were only indebted to the bank for some £20 5s. 7d., this to a great extent was through the large amount received for transfers, namely £1,311 6s. 3d., Charlie Roberts being the artist to bring the bulk in. However galling it was to see such a good man leave it can truly be said this was the salvation of the Club. Strange to say there seemed to be a unanimous feeling that it was possible to carry the Club on with success, and certainly the keynote was struck when Messrs. F. B. Coulson, W. H. Bellamy, and Rushworth consented to continue in office. Possibly the most sensible idea was the raising of the Directorate to fifteen with power to add. The following were elected to increase the Directorate — Messrs. Thompson, Bascomb, Brusey, Lacey, Green, Metcalf, Brown, Goodwin, F. Lacy, H. Dickinson, Doig and Cronshaw. Having cleared the atmosphere somewhat, preparations were made for the ensuing campaign, and when Barnsley were met at Blundell Park the following team was placed in the field: Spendiff, McConnell, A. McConnell, McDiarmid, Coles, Nelmes, Reynolds, Baker, Morley, Turner and Ross. Of the above, of course, Morley was the star artiste, out of his proper position as centre forward. As a matter of fact, quite by accident he found a true one, back, and to this day he occupies the position with Notts. County. On paper the Team looked strong enough, but the record at the new year was only moderate. Here it is :—

Matches				Goals		
Played	Won	Drawn	Lost	For	Against	Points
18	6	4	8	16	31	16

One of the most noteworthy items in the football world was the floating of Hull City as a Limited Company. This was the third attempt to establish Association football in the Third Port. Negotiations were opened with the Hull Rugby Football Association for a joint tenancy of their ground, and several matches were played there, but dissension speedily arose, and the result was that arrangements were made with the Hull City Cricket Club to rent a section of their Anlaby Road ground, which eventually was leased and is destined to be their home for a considerable time according to present appearances. For a first season they had not half a bad team, at all events they were good enough to beat Grimsby twice. A bit rough, wasn't it? Against us they placed the following in the field :— Whitehouse, Brookes, Jones, Machin, Woolfe, Raisbeck, Rushton, Smith, Howe, Spence and Wilkinson.

This season we were exempted until the final round of the Qualifying Round, meeting Gainsborough Trinity, who were beaten two to none. The luck of the draw in the Competition Proper was not exactly in our favour, having to meet Stoke away. An excursion was run, express both ways, slightly different to the last time I visited Stoke, away back some ten years, when we came home switched on to a coal train. Although the Town were relieved of any further anxiety re the Competition the gate was very satisfactory and the exchequer received a much needed lift.

This was the season when Mr. W. H. Bellamy had the honour of being selected as linesman for the Final Tie of the English Cup between Aston Villa and Newcastle United at the Crystal Palace. Our old centre forward, "Tich" Appleyard, of Meg's Isle, was very confident that Newcastle would win, and he would possess the height of every footballer's ambition, the gold medal, but life is full of disappointments, and he had his this journey, as Aston Villa knocked the favourites out somewhat easily.

In the Lincolnshire Cup' the Town had anything but a brilliant record. Exempted from the Qualifying Round, with Gainsborough Trinity and Lincoln City, they were drawn in the semi final with the Grimsby Rangers. To everybody's surprise, including their own, they had the greatest difficulty in making a draw. At the second attempt they won easily, but in the final failed to extend Gainsborough Trinity, who, by way of a change, became holders of the trophy.

As the season advanced the form shown was distinctly bad, and gates as a consequence dropped practically to zero. Whatever the cause was the Team was certainly better value than the following record shows, although in justice to them it should be stated they lost no less than three positions by goal average, which is one more proof of the value of notching goals at every opportunity. Position 13th.

Matches				Goals		
Played	Won	Drawn	Lost	For	Against	Points
34	11	8	15	33	49	30

At the close season of course the Directorate were once more faced with the Summer wages problem, and various other items, which most certainly had to be dealt with in the immediate future. At a meeting of shareholders held at the Royal Hotel various suggestions were made, such as holding a bazaar, etc. To suggest is the easiest thing in the world, but if the parties offering it had experienced just a little of the work, worry, etc., attending the promotion perhaps they would not have been so keen in advancing this theory to raise the all necessary. As a matter of fact experience taught me, and undoubtedly everybody who had been behind the scenes, that the bulk of the revenue that accrued to the funds of the Club generally was either of the gifts in kind or money from the various Directors and a few friends who

THE BOOT MAN.

I STAND BEHIND EVERY PAIR I SELL.

POWELL, THE BOOT MAN,
STRAND STREET, GRIMSBY.

happened to be at the helm.

One of the most important meetings ever held in connection with the League was held this Summer. As mentioned frequently in these pages, the relegation and promotion of clubs in the First and Second Divisions had been more or less a scandal for several years, and just now it reached a climax. The natural result was that some drastic scheme had to be advanced to avert the inevitable split, and it was decided to increase both divisions to twenty clubs. By this decision, of course, the two bottom clubs of the First Division retained their position, and the two top clubs of the Second Division were promoted to the upper house. This, of course, necessitated four new clubs being selected for the Second Division, and after a keen competition the following were elected :— Burton United, Hull City, Clapton Orient, and Stockport County. A rare slice of luck for our friends, Hull City, who, to a very great extent, had to thank the three Lincolnshire teams, Lincoln City, Gainsborough Trinity and Grimsby Town, for their promotion. Possibly the most noticeable absentee when the Town lined up for the first match was Spendiff in goal, who had been transferred to Hull City for the old reason. How he served them well for several seasons and then was transferred to Bradford City will easily be remembered by the followers of football of the present day. Cartledge, a local man, succeeded him. I never had the pleasure of being introduced to him, but I understand he is the son of an old comrade of mine in the old Worsley days, Sam Cartledge, the builder, who then frequently came to play for Notts. Commercials and other Nottingham teams. It seems but yesterday since Sam and I met on the cricket field, and yet Grimsby's goalkeeper was not then born. How time flies?

After the past disastrous season from a playing point of view, the general concensus of opinion was that at length the tide had turned. Why, I know not, for had not the Directorate to part with every pearl they possessed to keep afloat? As a matter of fact the results when the curtain rung down for half-time were very similar to last year. Here they are :— Position 8th.

Matches				Goals		
Played	Won	Drawn	Lost	For	Against	Points
19	7	6	6	21	20	20

It is consoling to note, as a casual glance will prove, that at all events the defence was all solid. Evidently it was the attack that required strengthening.

Naturally the general public, and also the Directorate, were anxiously awaiting the result of the draw for the competition proper of the English Cup. When it arrived, Newcastle United, at Grimsby, everybody was delighted in different ways. The public, with the idea that they would see at least one good Cup Tie during the season, and the Directorate, that just by way of a change, they had had a bit of luck, and a large amount of the all necessary was practically within their grasp. Very soon the secret leaked out, the Directorate were negotiating to play the match up in the North. At once the heavens assumed a luminous tint, but the Directorate were firm, and rightly so, as this policy alone could possibly keep the Club afloat. The precise terms were never divulged, but it is satisfactory to note that no less than £714 was taken at the gate, and there-fore the Town Directorate would get something approaching £450, a veritable godsend. Of the result, the less said the better. Our team was quite outclassed, and was decisively beaten, Appleyard, our old centre, particularly enjoying himself.

Shortly afterwards it was announced that a new lease had been secured from Mr. Alcock on favourable terms, and also that Messrs. J. H. Thompson, W. T. Green, and E. W. Lacey tendered their resignations as Directors, which were accepted. The former, as Chairman of Committee, had done any amount of spade work for the Club, and therefore fully deserved the thanks of all supporters for his efforts in securing a fresh lease, and also improving it from a financial point of view. In the new year, better form was shown by the team, West Bromwich Albion being among the victims.

In the Lincolnshire Cup, after the Cits. had once more been removed by the Town in the semi-final, Gainsborough Trinity went through the same operation in the final. It cannot be said that any amount of interest was taken now in the competition, neither will there ever be in the future as, since the inception of the League, these competitions can be numbered amongst the relics of the past.

It may be as well to note that Young, of Cleethorpes, was given a trial this season and did fairly well, but apparently was then, as now, just. lacking the necessary dash to play with clubs the calibre of the Town. As everybody knows he is now playing with Tottenham Hotspur, and I doubt whether the Directorate of the Town were quite justified in transferring him to Gainsborough Trinity.

Of course, there never was any great danger of the Town figuring in the last two when the figures were finally cast up, although they were several times on the fringe of it, but few of their supporters expected they would come with such a rattle at the finish and occupy the eighth position with the following record :—

Matches				Goals		
Played	Won	Drawn	Lost	For	Against	Points
38	15	 13	10	 46	46	 40

I was very much amused when I heard of the bombshell that had been hurled at Manchester United Club by the Football Association, and personally I cannot say I have any amount of sympathy for the directors, officials, or players either. Firstly, the former were only marionettes, tools in the hands of a certain party, who had the cool audacity to allow it to become common property that he was financing the club. This, of course, was directly against the interests of true football. Re the officials — early on in the season it would have paid them to run down to this district by a day excursion and interview some of the old crowd. They might easily have got a tip or two of how the oracle was worked in the days of veiled professionalism, when it was necessary to have a double set of books. As far as the players were concerned it was quite time the effectual stopper was put on, and their fines and suspensions were quite in order, as, if this had been allowed, it would have been simply impossible for clubs like Grimsby Town to have kept afloat.

When the annual meeting of the Town Club was held the patrons who attended were provided with the usual deluge of figures re the balance sheet, which eventually was adopted. Some very pertinent questions were asked re the grand stand by one of the leading officials of the Club. Perhaps the answers were satisfactory, or perhaps not, but at all events they cleared the atmosphere somewhat, which was required more than a little just then. Once more resignation being the order of the day, Messrs. W. H. Bellamy and Rushworth both tendered theirs, which were accepted, a matter much to be regretted, especially so far as the former was concerned. For years he had been doing any amount of work in the interests of the Club, both at home and away, but it was ever thus. A good man's services never are appreciated until they are lost, and this was a case in point.

1906-7.

Having been exempted from the qualifying rounds, and the team strengthened in its supposed weak places, the prospects seemed somewhat brighter when the curtain was rung up for this season. The old favourites, Notts. Forest, were the bill of fare. A large crowd assembled, and what is more satisfactory the Town won by a substantial margin of three to one. The following represented the Town :—

Goal, Cartledge.
Backs, Morley and McDonald.
Half backs, McGregor, Milnes and Higgins.
Forwards, Rodgers, Robinson, Hakin, Morris and Swarbrick.

It cannot be said that the form shown by the Team in the first half of the season was satisfactory. Indeed, it was not, but allowance should be made for the calibre of the teams comprising the League. Certanly just now they were stronger than they had ever been. Here they are :—

Notts. Forest.	Leicester Fosse.
Bradford City.	Burnley.
Hull City.	Fulham,
Leeds City.	Blackpool.
Burslem Port Vale.	Lincoln City.
Chelsea.	West Bromwich Albion.
Wolverhampton Wanderers.	Barnsley.
Grimsby Town.	Stoke.
Stockport County.	Clapton Orient.
Chesterfield.	Burton United.

Even then the following record was very poor :—

Matches				Goals		
Played	Won	Drawn	Lost	For	Against	Points
20	7	2	11	25	33	16

Once more charity was in the air. This time on the football field, and thanks to the efforts of Bill Cox and Charlie Daley, quite a substantial sum was gathered in. Re the play, I did not notice that any of the English Selection Committee were present on the look out for a budding Bloomer, but I did notice the chaffing division was present from the Pontoon, and apparently they enjoyed themselves immensely.

The Directorate had no cause for complaint of the draw in the competition proper, as Woolwich Arsenal were down as the bill of fare at Blundell Park. Nothing could fairly be better, as not only were they of sufficient class to draw the public, but there was more than an outside chance of beating them. Of course, ambassadors duly arrived with the idea of inducing the Town to play the match down South, but this journey they had a fruitless errand. It is satisfactory to note that the general public practically filled the enclosure, the turnstiles ticking merrily to the tune of £487. The result, a tie, perhaps, disappointing from a playing point of view, in other respects was a blessing in disguise, for did we not share another gate of £457; not bad this, for an off day. The following team represented the Town :—

Goal, Carmichael.
Backs, Morley and Butler.
Half-backs, McGregor, T. Morris and Higgins.
Forwards, Hooper, Rodgers, Burnett, R. Morris and Swarbrick.

This was not the only slice of luck from a pecuniary point of view, as later on in the season something approaching £600 was gathered in for three weeks' fixtures, and yet the season financially was not a success. What on earth would have happened with a bad draw in the Cup and bad weather at Easter is not difficult to guess. In fact it would have landed the Town in a hopeless position. This could only point one way, namely, that in respect to the all necessary at this period the Club was metaphorically sitting on a volcano and retrenchment in a wage point of view was absolutely a necessity.

Evidently this was the opinion of more than one Director, as Messrs. Goodwin, J. Doig and Cronshaw expressed a desire to resign. It was surmised in some quarters that Messrs. Bellamy and Rushworth might be induced to reconsider their decision and join the Board, but they were not having any, neither do I blame them.

Although they lost the final of the Lincolnshire Cup, Gainsborough doing the needful, they showed much improved form in the League as the season advanced, and their position when the curtain finally descended was not at all bad. Here it is :—

Matches				Goals		
Played	Won	Drawn	Lost	For	Against	Points
38	16	3	19	57	62	35

1907-8.

When the annual meeting was held at the Oberon Hotel, Mr. W. Goodwin being in the chair, we had the usual deluge of figures. How lovely they can be made on paper, but the gaunt spectre of Summer wages was still a reality. Why men of business throughout the country should sacrifice their time, and also be liable for large sums of money, is only another instance of their inherent love of the game, but depend upon it, sooner or later drastic steps will have to be taken if the minor lights of the football world, in which I class both the Cits. and Trinitarians, are not to become relics of the past.

During the Summer holidays team building was indulged in, the most satisfactory recruits being Wheelhouse, who has indeed been a find, and Vincett, one of the numerous artistes who excel both at cricket and football. Of course, it is well known that he got his County cap for Sussex, which proves his merit as regards the smaller ball, but after all, the larger is the one we are most concerned with, and he speedily proved he was anything but a novice in the back position. When the opening match was played against the Cits., it was practically a new team which took the field, but ere long not a few had to take a back seat, a matter inevitable on the form shown.

Throughout the season the form in the League was most unsatisfactory. Why, is a difficult problem to solve. Perhaps some of the Team were riding for a fall, a rather fashionable pastime with not a few so-called stars, who by this means often get transferred sooner than they would have done in the ordinary course of events. However, apparently the Team was too good to suffer the degradation of having to apply for re-election to the League, and yet this was the fate of Grimsby Town when the figures were finally cast up. Here they are :—

Matches				Goals			
Played	Won	Drawn	Lost	For	Against	Points	
38	11	8	19	43	72	30	

Luckily their previous record, and the form shown in the English Cup were sufficient to cause their re-election at the head of the poll, with Chesterfield second and Bradford third, in the place of Lincoln City. Everybody in the Fisheries regretted the throwing out of the Cits., but it was only the shadow on the blind of what eventually happened to Grimsby Town, namely the power of the almighty dollar, which alone caused Bradford to have this preference.

When Stoke resigned there yet appeared a chance for the Cits., but once more the almighty dollar played its part very well, and Tottenham Hotspur were elected. It was not without a struggle, however, as Grimsby Town and others fought hard for the Cits., but after they had tied twice it was left to the management Committee of the League to decide, and the Hotspurs had the preference.

In the midst of all the trouble caused by the bad form in the League, few imagined the Team was destined to have such a brilliant career in the English Cup Ties. When the news came that the Town were drawn against Bristol City in the First Round away a speedy exit was expected, but it wasn't, oh dear no. They tied, and what is more satisfactory, won on the replay. Carlisle United proved ready victims in the Second Round by six goals to two, three of these goals being scored in about as many minutes. Truly a thrilling finish. In the Third Round they ran up against some stronger talent, at home again, Crystal Palace to wit, but after a tremendous struggle one goal was notched, the best for some time, for did it not possess the intrinsic value of no less than £700. Blanthorne did this good turn for the Town. In the last eight naturally they got amongst the cream of the talent, very luckily being drawn against Newcastle United away from home. Just now, of course, there was any amount of excitement knocking about in the Fisheries, excursions were run; no less than 1,000 making the journey. As generally expected the Novocastrians proved a barrier to Cup honours, and decisively too, the margin being five to one. Appleyard was the artiste that did the damage.

As a result of the Cup Ties, the secretary and treasurer, in fact all the officers, donned double-six smiles, and well they might, when they surveyed these lovely figures :—

		£	s.	d
1st Round	Bristol City at Bristol	324	0	0
	Replay at Grimsby	203	18	4
2nd Round	Carlisle United at Grimsby	244	0	0
3rd Round	Crystal Palace at Grimsby	524	0	0
4th Round	Newcastle United at Newcastle	1,582	12	6
		2,878	10	10

Truly it was a veritable godsend, especially as Blanthorne showed form good enough to cause Newcastle to give a substantial figure for his transfer. After all this is only another instance of the Cup Ties coming to the rescue of the Club when in difficulties, and it will be a catastrophe to any club if the interest in the Cup Ties should become a thing of the past, but this idea is too absurd to contemplate for one moment.

It was a capital idea to play a Veterans' match between the old players of Lincoln City and Grimsby Town, home and home, for the benefit of the charities, as it was the means of those players of bygone days renewing acquaintance, and also enjoying themselves more than a little at the tea held after the match. The match at Lincoln was won by the Cits., but the Town whipped up a stronger lot for the return, but only made a draw of it. The following were the teams :—

GRIMSBY TOWN. — George Atkinson, J. Lundie, J. H. Taylor, secretary, Bob Gray, Cob Smith, T. Atkinson, Bob McBeth, Jack Taylor, T. Soames, J. Rodgers, J. Chapman.

LINCOLN CITY. — Kenny Eaynes, W. Rawlinson, W. Jeffrey, T. Palm, W. Richardson, W. Simpson, E. Metham, J. Rainey, J. Irving, H. C. Simpson, F. Smallman.

1908-9.

Although Blanthorne had migrated to Newcastle the return of Appleyard and the arrival of Leonard, etc., pointed, if anything, to the Town being much stronger this season, but strange to say the form shown throughout was extremely moderate, both in League and Cup Ties. Why, it is difficult to imagine, especially when an eye is cast upon the following players that were available :— Scott, Wheelhouse, Bradley, Birkinshaw, Henderson, Lee, Davidson, Hatton, Ripley, Springthorpe, Owers, Coxon, Kilbourne, Stokes, Beadling, Appleyard, Satterthwaite, Leonard and Kelly. For some time it really appeared as if they would once more be applicants for reinstatement, but this disgrace was saved. In fact, they finished thirteenth with the following record :—

Matches				Goals		
Played	Won	Drawn	Lost	For	Against	Points
38	14	7	17	41	54	35

Just by way of a change this season it was arranged to play the Lincoinshire Cup Ties early on, and the Town, having relieved Gainsborough Trinity of any further anxiety re the pot, proceeded to administer the usual order of the knock to the Cits., and won the Cup, about the only ray of sunshine they enjoyed during this disastrous season.

In the English Cup the hopes of the partizans of the Club ran high when they.were drawn at home against Stockport County, but strange to say the Team quite failed to realise expectation and after drawing at the first attempt were quite overplayed in the second, deserving the loss. Financially this result was nothing short of a calamity to Grimsby Town, and once more the bird began to whistle, and not a very lively tune either.

During the close season the frictions between the various directorates and the Players' Union became very acute. In fact it was only by a great amount of tact shown by Veitch, of Newcastle, that an open breach was averted. It is not my intention to go into the merits of the case, but I do know for a certainty that not one club in ten can stand the pressure of the current rate of wages, and others besides Grimsby Town must have been literally wiped off the map if it had not been for the great help financially they have received from the English Cup Competition.

This year the Grimsby Rangers joined the Amateur Alliance League, and more than held their own in the Competition, beating strong teams like Sheffield Grasshoppers, Leicester Nomads, etc. Unfortunately they were terribly handicapped by the position of the ground, it being situated on Yarborough Road, the greatest drawback being the impossibility of charging a gate, owing to it being quite open to the road. It was suggested to go round with the hat, but alas, it scarcely required a Chancellor of the Exchequer to check the takings, with the result that the Club must have been a very heavy burden upon the few enthusiasts who ran it.

1909-10.

The most disastrous year Grimsby Town ever experienced from a playing point of view. From the very first the Team appeared utterly unable to make an effort, with the result that when half time arrived on January 1st, they were absolutely at the bottom of the League, a position nothing short of disgraceful when they had something like thirty-four players at their command, all of whom were supposed to be capable men. During the first half of the season they were guilty of the following record :—

Matches				Goals		
Played	Won	Drawn	Lost	For	Against	Points
22	3	3	16	18	50	9

Even now there was a possible chance to escape degradation, but it was not to be, and when the curtain was rung down they finished second from the bottom. True, with a little luck, even at the last hurdle, the match at Gainsborough the situation might have been saved, but the effort was too late, and their record ran thus :—

Matches				Goals		
Played	Won	Drawn	Lost	For	Against	Points
38	9	6	23	54	77	24

Just for a tonic, when the final of the Lincolnshire Cup was played, our dear friends, the Cits., took the liberty of rubbing it in by no less than four goals to nil, slightly different to the form in the old days. I can imagine the jubilation in the Cathedral City on that night.

For years the English Cup Competition had been relied upon. to supply a large proportion of the all necessary, and few will deny that Grimsby Town had not enjoyed a certain amount of luck in gathering it in during its career, but this season they came a veritable cropper at the first hurdle. When Bristol Rovers were drawn here we naturally expected to reach the Second Round, but it was not to be, as the western team won easily. To fill the cup to the brim the General Election was fixed for this day, and the result was the gate was the smallest on record, a paltry £125.

If ever a Directorate deserved sympathy surely it was Grimsby Town at this period. With the bird assuming the dimensions of an eagle and the extreme probability of not being re-elected in the Second Division, they were indeed having a lively time. However, to their credit they faced the situation boldly, but in vain, as Huddersfield were elected, and Grimsby relegated to the Midland League. How this was done does not require a Solomon to solve, as the problem is very easy. Once more the almighty dollar! Clearly it was not a case of merit, as the new aspirants had not only been beaten by the Town Reserves, but also held a very moderate position when the Midland League was cast up. Early on the shadow was cast on the

blind, for did not the one and only official of the League busy himself in recommending the Huddersfield ground for International matches. However, it was no good crying over the matter. A gross injustice had been done to Grimsby Town, and a determined effort had to be made to secure the Championship of the Midland League, the stepping-stone to re-election.

Perhaps a brief resume of Grimsby Town's record up-to-date may be of some interest to the budding enthusiast of the present period. Since they joined the Alliance, they repeatedly held a good position, and when the League was formed, of course, were elected to the Second Division. For years they had the hardest of luck in missing the test matches, but after these were abolished, to the delight of all their supporters they secured the Championship of the Second Division in 1900, and, of course, were elected to the upper house. They only held this for two years. Why? Simply because they were rushed out by a series of the most glaring frauds ever perpetrated in the history of football. Although some of the officials that participated in it were warned off the football fields for ever Grimsby Town had to accept the inevitable, and once more figured in the Second Division. When this catastrophe happened the supporters little thought after eight seasons they would get another lower, but the fact is there all the same, and very unpalatable it is.

1910-11.

Re the financial portion of the business, the transfer of Scott to Everton eased the pressure a little, and the bird recovered somewhat, so the policy of the Directorate was still progressive, and a capable team was secured for season 1910-11. Although the clouds were dark enough in all conscience, the chances were that financially it might be a better season as, firstly, a determined effort was to be made in the English Cup Competition, and secondly the probability was that with a winning team in the Midland League the public would rally round the Club in greater numbers than hitherto.

From the commencement it was very evident that business was meant, and a determined effort would be made to obtain the Championship, but there were several powerful reserve teams, such as Sheffield Wednesday Reserves, and the chances were that the struggle would be much keener than anticipated in some quarters. At half-time they were third with the following record to their credit :—

Matches				Goals		
Played	Won	Drawn	Lost	For	Against	Points
19	12	4	 3	 54	18	 28

As the termination of the season approached the contest became much keener, indeed it was not until practically the last fixture that Grimsby Town secured the Championship with the following fine record :—

Matches				Goals		
Played	Won	Drawn	Lost	For	Against	Points
38	25	7	 6	 94	32	 57

If for nothing else this season saw quite a revival in English Cup Tie fever in this district. In the competition proper the Town had the luck to be drawn against Croydon Common, of the Southern League, who were decisively beaten. To everybody's surprise, however, the Football Association on a very frivolous protest, ordered it to be replayed. This journey the Town rubbed it in by no less than eight goals to one. Drawn against Crewe Alexandra away, an unknown quantity, the chances appeared slightly against them, but they confounded the critics and won easily enough, thus entering into the Third Round. Once more they were away, against the team destined to win the Cup, namely, Bradford City. Unfortunately for the Town, Leonard, the centre-forward, was suspended at the time, which materially weakened the team, and although the Meg Islander, Young, played, the absence of Leonard was keenly felt. Indeed with some the idea was prevalent that we might have won with his assistance, but alas, it was not to be, but on the other hand we had the consolation of finally being beaten by the ultimate winners of the cup, and secondly sharing in a good gate.

With the Championship of the Midland League, and their performances in the Cup Ties, the Directorate had every confidence that they would be re-elected to the Second Division of the League, but nevertheless recognised that the Cits., represented by my old friend John Henry, would make a determined effort, and they were quite correct in their surmising, as they only beat the Cits. by the odd vote. Who gave this odd vote is an open question, the Wolves, Bury, and Sheffield United all claiming that they gave the Town the preference over Lincoln City. Whether they did or no is quite immaterial to us, but to a certainty had it not been for their efforts and my old friend, Jack Whitsed, and Harry Hickson, the secretary, who devoted ten days to canvassing the Clubs, travelling 1,812 miles and the final touch given by Sir George Doughty in his eloquent speech at the general meeting, we should have been doomed to another season in the Midland League, which possibly might have wrecked the Club.

SEASON 1911-12.

To all appearances this was to be the second time on earth re the Grimsby Town Club in the League, and determined efforts were made by the Directors to place a team on the field qualified to more than hold its own against the average Second League team. Have they succeeded? is the question of the hour. Personally I think they have, and if the results are not quite so satisfactory as anticipated in some quarters, this may be attributed to the fact that they have been extremely unlucky, to put it mildly, in some of the decisions given against them, which have meant a sufficient loss of points to have placed them in the danger zone for positions in the upper house. Considering they have succeeded in finishing well in the upper half of the Table in a Division admittedly stronger than it has ever been before, the form shown is satisfactory, particularly in the away matches, where the following draws were made — Birmingham, Burnley and Barnsley, a fine trio, whilst wins were notched at the expense of Leicester Fosse, Blackpool, Leeds City, Wolverhampton Wanderers, Gainsborough and Fulham. The one fly in the ointment was that record namely, their defeat by Lincoln City in the English Cup. For about thirty years the Cits. had been trying to win an English Cup Tie against the Town, so naturally my old friend, J. H. S., would be jubilant. Personally I don't begrudge him the honour, but the consequences were far-reaching from a financial point of view, and it says much for the Directorate that they were able to stand such a disaster at the critical period of the season. Remarks like the above may cause surprise, but they need not, as I can assure all from personal experience that the clubs that can afford to be beaten in the 1st Round of the English Competition can be counted on the fingers of one hand, as the whole of them at one time or other have been rescued from financial chaos by the almighty dollars that have accrued from English Cup-Ties. The following is the record for the season :— Position 9th.

Photo by]   [Lowthian Bros., Grimsby.

GRIMSBY TOWN F.C. TEAM, 1911-12.

Matches				Goals		
Played	Won	Drawn	Lost	For	Against	Points
38	15	14	9	48	55	39

It was satisfactory to note that already the nucleus of a powerful team had been signed for next season, and I should imagine the followers of Grimsby Town can rest assured that with the capable Directorate the Town Club has at present, and a secretary like Harry Hickson, who knows the inner workings of the game from A to Z, there will be little danger of the Town ever having to go cap in hand again to obtain re-election to the Second Division.

It is with a pang of regret that on the very eve of the finish of this book I should hear of the death of yet another comrade of the old Brigade. I allude to Aaron Burnham. For a period of some 35 years as member, player and director he has figured in the annals of Grimsby Town. How prominent a part he played in the development of the Winter pastime it is impossible to imagine, but to a certainty, knowing him during the whole of this period, the value of his services both financially and otherwise must have been enormous. Cool, quiet, unassuming yet firm, he was a born leader of men, not easily lead astray by rash calculations, and it says much for him that despite the great responsibility attending the position as director of a football club, Aaron still was willing, and did stand his corner through the various vicissitudes experienced, by Grimsby Town. Even in the darkest hour he always was optimistic, and if there is one consolation it is a pleasure to note that he lived long enough to see Grimsby Town once more figure in the League. Possibly it will be the youngsters who will feel his loss the most. Yes, if ever a man did take a delight in teaching the rising generation manly pastimes it was Aaron Burnham, and now alas, he is gone, one of the best.

It may be interesting to append four teams of various periods of Grimsby Town's career. Which is the best? Like old "Prosser," in the Queen's Head Yard when Napoleon was crossing the Alps, I say, "Which you like, my little dears." It is a knotty problem.

TEAM 1887.

Goal, Houltby.

Backs, Lundie and Doyle.

Half-backs, J. H. Taylor, H. Smith, W. Reid.

Forwards, J. Lee, D. Sutherland, D. Riddock, R. McBeth, J. Hunt..

TEAM 1892.

Goal, Whitehouse.

Backs, Lundie and Langley.

Half-backs, Higgins, W. Reid, A. Ogilvie.

Forwards, A. Rose, Fletcher, McCairns, McKnight, Black.

TEAM 1902.

Goal, Whittaker.

Backs, Mountain and Leiper.

Half-backs, Hemingfield, Bellingham and Nelmes.

Forwards, Dean, Harper, Appleyard, Ronaidson, and Gardner.

TEAM 1911-12.

Goal, Lonsdale.

Backs, Wheelhouse and Arrowsmith.

Half-backs, Browell, Gordon and Martin.

Forwards, Staniforth, Hubbard, Mounteney, Mayson and Worth.

I do know, however, which is the best front line which ever donned the.
Town's colours. Here it is :—

Riddock, Lee, Geary, McBeth and Cooper.

I wonder what this quintette would be worth in the market today.

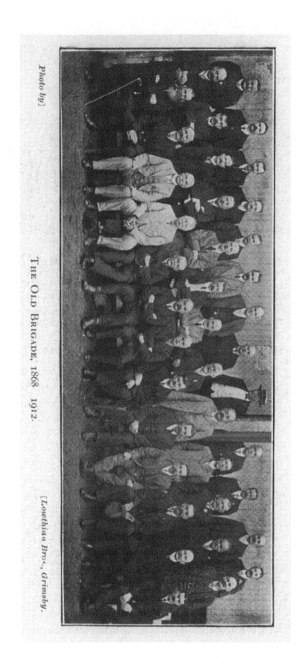

Photo by]

The Old Brigade, 1868 1912.

(Louthian Bros., Grimsby.

145

JUNIOR FOOTBALL.

Throughout the whole of the career of Grimsby Town the Juniors of the District have occasionally been called upon to wear the colours, but I for one have always had the idea that their services were never utilised to the extent they might have been. There is an old saying that a prophet is without honour in his own country, and this clearly applies to football, as it is simply remarkable how a strange Club swoops down and fetches a valuable recruit from under the very eyes, as it were, of those in command of the leading club in the district. Taking a casual glance backward, if any further proof were required of the value of junior teams, let us remember that players the calibre of Appleyard, Cob Smith, the Friths, the Murrells, the Roses, Hopewell, Bodge Mountain, Young, Blanchard, etc., have more than held their own in the best of company and why should there not be valuable recruits. available at the present time. True, I am aware, the pace is a cracker, it is absolutely necessary that the man secured should be fully qualified, but all the same, considering a Midland League Team is run, I don't think the powers that be quite give the juniors of the town a chance. Re those bygone days, I cannot close these columns without a reference. For the last thirty years we have always had good teams knocking about in the Fisheries. Here are a few :— Humber Rovers, Perseverance, Cleethorpes, in the old days, and now we possess teams the calibre of Haycroft Rovers, Cleethorpes and the Rovers, possibly almost up to Midland League form. Clearly the rising generation have reason to thank the pioneers of this branch of sport, such as W. H. Bellamy, Aaron Burnham, Chris. White, Charlie Parker, C. Willmer, J. Plastow, and others I could mention. At the present moment, if any further proof were required of the strength of junior football, may I mention the astounding fact that no less than 29 clubs are affiliated to the Lincolnshire Association. Naturally some of them are not particularly strong, but still it is quite on the cards that at least three clubs, namely Cleethorpes, Haycroft Rovers, and Grimsby Rovers, which, I understand, have all entered the English Cup Competition, may easily effect a surprise by defeating teams of a greater reputation in the football world. Another item worth noticing is the formation of the Grimsby and District Referees' Association. In the old days, we had no examination to undergo, although, let it be known, we did not exactly profess to be novices in the understanding of the offside rule.

Still, no doubt, it was absolutely necessary for all those behind the whistle to have the courage of their convictions, or shall I say, not care a big D—— for either the players or, spectators in a far greater degree than in the present day, as, clearly, they were not protected by the drastic rules that are now in force. At the request of several I append a list of Junior Clubs, and likewise the secretaries.

Junior Clubs, affiliated to the Lincolnshire Association.

DIVISION I.

Cleethorpes Town — E. Prowse, 89, St. Peter's Avenue.

Grimsby Rovers — W. H. Moody, 199, Willingham Street.

Haycroft Rovers — H. Little, 31, Haycroft Street.

Humber Rovers — F. Storey, 226, Victoria Street.

St. John's — E. George, 121, Oxford Street.

DIVISION II.

Albion Works — E. A. Wilks, 401, Weelsby Street.

Celtic — W. Stone, 139, Brereton Avenue.

Cleethorpes Town — E. Prowse, 89, St. Peter's Avenue.

Cleethorpes Victoria — H. Osborne, 89, Thrunscoe Road.

Grimsby Amateurs — W. Capps, 13, Vere Terrace.

Grimsby Liberals — J. H. Smith, 120, Lord Street.

Grimsby Rovers 2nd. — W. H. Moody, 199, Willingham Street.

Hainton Amateurs — C. Turner, 27, Eastgate.

N.I.C. — H. Parkin, 53, Edward Street.

St. John's 2nds. — E. W. George, 121, Oxford Street.

St. Paul's — E. R. Binnington, 71, Hainton Avenue.

Tickler's Works — F. Hallett, 82, Legsby Avenue.

DIVISION III.

Alexandra United — C. Taylor, 390, Wellington Street.

All Saints — C. Jackson, 33, Eleanor Street.

Cromwell Adelaide — C. Cuthbert, 212, Convamore Road.

Electricity Works — A. Nuttall, 36, Thorold Street.

Grimsby Trinity — A. P. Robinson, 22, Chantry Lane.

Grimsby United — C. Johnson, 19, Flower Square.

Humberstone — J. C. Smith, Wireless Telegraph Station.

Oxford Mission — W. Watkinson, 328, Clayton Street.

St. Barnabas — A. Garlick, 110, Hainton Avenue.

Scartho — C. Saynor, 171, Hainton Avenue.

Tickler's Works 2nd — F. Hallett, 82, Legsby Avenue.

Victoria United — G. Allen, 95, Ravenspurn Street.

GRIMSBY AND DISTRICT REFEREES' ASSOCIATION.
HEADQUARTERS, RAILWAY HOTEL.

Chairman, W. H. Moody.

Hon. Secretary, W. Coultas, 17, Park View, Tiverton Street.

J. J. Abbott, 31, Suggitt's Lane, Cleethorpes.

L. Backhouse, 13, Augustin Street, Grimsby.

A. E. Barker, 133, Fairmont Road, Grimsby.

A. Parker, 6, Augustin Street, Grimsby.

P. R. Binnington, 66, Legsby Avenue, Grimsby.

J. Canty, 89, Edward Street, Grimsby.

W. Coultas, 17, Park View, New Cleethorpes.

J. Darley, 47, Weelsby Street, Grimsby.

H. Darley, 355, Convamore Road, Grimsby.

C. Daws, Ravenspurn Street, Grimsby.

A. Dawson, Haven Terrace, Grimsby.

J. H. Denniss.

W. Egleton, Elsenham Road, Little Coates.

J. Gibbins, 42, Rutland Street, Grimsby.

E. Gooseman, 31, Freeston Street, New Cleethorpes.

F. Hooton, 29, Convamore Road, Grimsby.

W. Hooton, 246, Freeman Street, Grimsby.

G. Hobbins.

G. Hubbard, 54, Granville Street, Grimsby.

A. E. W. May, Cleethorpe Road, Grimsby.

W. H. Moody, 199, Willingham Street, Grimsby.

W. Mastin, 17 Spencer Street, New Clee.

H. Middleton, 39, Coombe Street, New Cleethorpes.

E. Prowse, St. Peter's Road, Cleethorpes.

— Pearson, 100, Bentley Street, Cleethorpes.

J. Shepperdson, 37, Peaksfield Avenue, Grimsby.

J. Smith, 120, Lord Street, Grimsby.

A. Thompson, 71, Chapman Street, Grimsby.

D. Walker, 1, Blundell Avenue, New Cleethorpes.

C. Watkinson, 18, Cleethorpe Road, Grimsby.

J. Willing, Spencer Street, Grimsby.

FINIS.